***INSIDE*** - *Learn the comi*
*and techniques that will m*
*as well as long term su*

# NLP
## Next Level
# PERSUASION

*SELL anything to anyone*
*and have them thank you for it!*

# DAN STOREY

For permission requests, contact the author at www.nextlevelpersuasion.com.
Graphic design & layout: Go-Enki.com

ISBN 978-0-9929534-0-9

Next Level Persuasion: How to sell anything to anyone and have them thank you for it. / Dan Storey.

# TABLE OF CONTENTS

# INTRODUCTION

Today, the image of the traditional salesperson is probably at its lowest point in history. Despite it being the most essential job in any business, responsible for generating the revenue which pays every other department's salaries, when you ask people for their opinion on sales people, what do you hear? Tricky. Conniving. Untrustworthy. Only out for themselves. Sound familiar?

How did sales get such a bad reputation? Well the problem is there is no smoke without fire. In the past, this 'hit-and-run' approach to sales worked. Think about the traveling salesperson who knocks on your door, offering to sell you new windows or better gas and electricity prices. What about the car salesperson that greets you with a smile as you timidly walk on to the forecourt in search of your new vehicle? What about the insurance salesperson who talks all about how great their products are and how no-one else in the marketplace even comes close?

We used to buy from these people; we had to. If you wanted insurance, you had to go to your local insurance salesperson. If you wanted better utilities prices, you had to trust that the person who knocked on your door would deliver on their promises.

The problems only ever started after the sale had been made.

As you drive your car off the forecourt, you smile at your partner in the passenger seat, eager and excited at all of the journeys that the two of you had planned to take in your new car. A day or two later, you notice a clunking noise coming from the engine. It seems pretty bad and the car is almost undriveable as a result, so you decide to go back to the salesperson that sold you the car. What happens next?

> *"It wasn't like that when you bought it. You must have done something to it. It isn't our fault! You should have bought the upgraded warranty package like I told you!"*
>
> *"Don't talk to me, I'm just the sales person. It's not my problem now, you need to talk to the service team. I'm too busy with someone else."*
>
> *"Him? Oh he doesn't even work here any more. What, you saw him hiding around the corner? No, that's not possible, he left over a week ago? Oh he sold you the car two days ago? Errr..."*

Now these may seem like extreme examples but these situations happen on sales floors across the world in every kind of business, not just used cars (although they do seem to have one of the worst reputations of all).

There is an opinion among consumers that sales people are only interested in getting the deal - earning their commission before turning their back on the way to their next potential victim. What happens if there is a question or concern after the sale is made? Well that certainly isn't the sales person's role. The sale was perfect. Any subsequent challenges can be dealt with by support.

Guess what... this worked! Sales people could become successful by following these approaches, so much so that they became the preferred sales model for some industries. If you buy double glazed windows today, the sales pitch is the same as the business was using 20 years ago (it might even be the same salesperson!).

Relative success plus continual education and perpetuation of these sales approaches ingrained this model into not just the sales industry, but also the minds of everyone that was ever sold to by such a salesperson. The sales person of yesterday was interested in quick wins and big commissions and they never looked back.

Then something happened - the world started getting smaller. And better informed. The power shifted in favour of the customer.

With a smaller world came competition, something which local businesses were not always positioned to cope with. Customers started asking the questions "why should I buy from you when I can get the same service from another town?" or "what are you going to throw in because I can get it cheaper on the Internet?".

Also, the Internet put all of the world's information into the palm of our hands. A salesperson makes a claim and before you know it, the prospect has Googled that very fact and has all of the research up on their screen. Plus, some smart companies started to put together comparison sites so that you could instantly compare products and services across hundreds of companies, not just from the salesperson in front of you.

The Internet also gave disgruntled customers a voice through social media. Suddenly, if a salesperson or organisation was less than satisfactory in their delivery or follow through, social media allowed other prospects all around the world to be informed of this shortcoming. Plus, as it has been shown that 90% of consumers trust peer reviews, if those comments show up on forums or review sites, that is going to have yet another negative impact on that salesperson's chance of closing the deal.

Gradually this shift of power put the consumer in charge. After years of feeling as though they had been taken advantage of by salespeople, prospects started to change the rules. There would be no more win-lose deals where the salesperson gets their commission and the customer is left wanting. No, the future would be win-win at least, and in many cases, the deal would be weighted in favour of the customer.

For businesses, the term 'Lifetime Customer Value' suddenly held more importance. Before the shift, businesses who attracted a client normally had them for life. You had one mortgage broker that helped you buy yours and your children's houses. You would have one plumber that would do everything from fix the smallest leak to replace your entire central heating system. You would have one greengrocer that would keep you fed all year round.

However, the availability of options meant that if your level of service dropped even for a moment, the chances of your customer shopping around would go through the roof. Upset them enough (and sometimes once would be enough) and they would let their feet do the talking and start to use your competitor.

This paradigm shift in favour of the customer poses the old sales methodology a difficult question. Do you continue the way you are, winning deals upfront but waving goodbye to the lifetime value of the client? Or do you try to embrace change, forgo the short term rush of a big deal but win by developing a relationship with a client that lasts over a longer period of time, eventually dwarfing the potential value of that initial sale?

Businesses have known about this shift for a while. There are some industries where the client relationship is so important that salespeople are being employed based on who they know and who they can bring to the table. No idea about our products? Don't worry, we can teach you all that, as long as you bring over Mr Smith from ABC Ltd. These salespeople with the contacts are able to negotiate better packages that even longstanding employees, and this is simply down to their ability to make a big impact right from their first day on the job. It seems that 'who' you know really is becoming more important than 'what' you know.

So are we moving into a beautiful utopia for salespeople? No more pressure to make that first sale as all our time and effort could be placed on developing relationships rather than the hard close. The prospect feels completely at ease with no pressure to buy and the salesperson seems generally interested in their needs and requirements. Surely then, this is the utopia we need to be cultivating? Isn't this the future of salesmanship as we know it? No sales targets, just qualitative information on how you are getting on with each of your prospects. No more pipeline, just questions about your network and contacts.

Knock knock. Who's there? The Real World!

Unfortunately, in developing this utopia, there would be an interim lag period during which no sales were made but lots of beautiful relationships were carefully created. If we were to apply this utopian approach to our work as salespeople today, tomorrow we would be looking for a new job.

Relationships would develop over time meaning we would miss our sales targets this month, maybe the next. Also, we could be developing relationships that may not even pay off for years and years.

In such a situation, salespeople would then be forced to start selecting relationships on the basis of likelihood of closing soon rather than genuine relationships irrespective of sales value. This would then lead us to prioritise the relationships with the highest possible value and the fastest possible time to close, We might even incentivise these new connections to get them to buy sooner.

Knock knock. Who's there? Someone who just went round in a circle!

Make no mistake, the future of sales is based around creating meaningful, valuable relationships. However, if you are to succeed as a salesperson today, and this will never change, you must be able to influence people to take action.

The new model of salesperson must embody both paradigms whilst maintaining complete integrity and ecology. The next level salesperson needs to know how to:

- Build relationships and influence rather than build relationships to influence.
- Help prospects make the right decision for them not the salesperson's commission.
- Be likeable as well as respected so that their advice is acted upon.

The problem salespeople face is that while businesses understand this shift, few of them are willing to invest in salespeople long enough for them to be able to develop these relationships purely organically. As soon as you join a sales organisation, your numbers are on the board for everyone to see. The pressure to close a deal and close it early is immediately apparent, no matter what words of encouragement your sales manager might impart. They want to know if they have invested in the right person to join their team, and if they don't think you are going to make it, it is almost as if you can hear each grain of sand dropping through the timer.

However, there is good news. We are entering the world of sales in a time where there is more opportunity than ever before. The majority of the salespeople that hold the existing relationships are still operating from the old paradigm and are at high risk of losing those customers to salespeople who understand the concepts of next level persuasion. More and more prospects are re-entering the marketplace in search of a supplier relationship with someone who views them more as a valuable client than a recurring commission cheque. This should excite you and every other salesperson as well as serve as a continual reminder to focus as much on service as you do on attracting new business. It is this balanced focus which makes Next Level Persuasion unique in the field of sales training.

Next Level Persuasion has utilised more than ten years of research and training to develop the models and teaching methods which now make it the invaluable resource it is for today's salespeople. This journey started after seeing a number of NLP (neuro-linguistic programming) trainers attempting to teach sales people the tools and techniques that exist within the toolbox of NLP.

Have you ever seen a child trying to figure out a shape sorter toy? You know the kind with the square, circle and star blocks with the appropriately shaped holes in the box? And have you ever seen the same child pick up the square block and try to use brute force to get it into the box through the wrong hole because it hadn't yet figured out how to choose the right piece for the right hole. This describes the result that a lot of these training courses had. I was just as guilty at the start.

I knew the techniques within NLP could significantly help salespeople in their challenge to influence their prospects into taking action. If they could just learn to adopt the techniques into their pitches, they would start to find themselves closing more deals, developing more rapport and being able to think faster on their feet when it came to questions and objection handling.

The problem was that none of the salespeople I met wanted to learn NLP. They were interested in learning how to sell, how to close and how to earn commission. This became highly evident about one and a half days into my first ever two-week sales training.

The feedback coming in was that the techniques were really interesting but how would this make them sell better? I was teaching NLP techniques with NLP names and the students wanted sales techniques with sales names. Something needed to change. If only I could teach sales techniques with sales names that were built upon the tools of NLP which would make them even more effective.

Over the next ten years, this is what I did. I worked with sales people from every industry I could find to learn their sales challenges so that I could then help them sell more effectively. Retail, business-to-business, selling from the stage and online sales copywriting all got pulled apart, deconstructed and then rebuilt from a foundation of techniques based on psychology, influence and neuro-linguistics. When it was finished, what had been created was Next Level Persuasion.

Realising that we are entering a new era of salesmanship, I promise this book will save you years of experimenting with tools and techniques that may or may not help your sales process. Everything in this book has been refined and applied in sales situations so that you know they work. I'll even give you examples of how to get it right (and also how it can go wrong) so that you can integrate the ideas immediately into your existing sales approach.

You will learn the concepts of Next Level Persuasion that allow you build strong, lasting relationships while selling and hitting your targets at the same time. You'll uncover the internal tricks that set you up for success as well as the linguistic patterns that will have your prospects agreeing with you and so motivated to take your product or service that you won't even need to close at the end of the sales meeting.

If you want a successful, lasting career in sales, keep reading. The ideas in this book will put you among the top performers in your industry and keep you there for a long, long time. If you are the person with the key relationships, this puts you in the driving seat, making you a valuable commodity for any business. Make no mistake about it, they will all be fighting to have you on their team. More than ever before, you, the salesperson holds the key to success in business. You pay the salaries of everyone else in the business, even the CEO.

The next level persuader is invaluable.

# CHAPTER 1
# THE NEW WORLD OF SALES

As businesses look to improve their cost effectiveness and profit margins, the salesperson is under ever-increasing scrutiny to produce results, and quickly. In a challenging economy, no business can afford to carry dead weight, especially if that person is supposed to be creating the revenue that will be paying the salaries of everyone else in the business.

And yet, who gets paid the higher commissions in a business? Typically, salespeople within a sales-focused organisation get paid very well, especially when they are performing.

This knife edge is both a blessing and a curse for salespeople. Succeed, and you will be lauded with praise and showered with expensive trinkets. Fail, and you become yet another person who has gone through the exit interview for your company. Ruthless or good business sense? That perspective depends entirely on how successful you have been as a salesperson.

So many businesses today churn through salespeople as if there exists an everlasting stream of candidates, and to some extent this is true. Sales has always been a role which attracted people with no other qualifications other than personality and the ability to communicate. It doesn't matter how well you did at school, if you can get people round to your way of thinking, you can get a job in sales.

What this means is that, for the successful salesperson, there will always be a job for you. Companies will always keep someone who can sell their product, no matter what is happening in the economy.

On the other hand, if you have no job right now, learn how to become a great salesperson. This will open up to you opportunities you may never have imagined and give you the opportunity to create the lifestyle of your dreams.

What if you own your own business? Do you think being an excellent salesperson would help? Of course, it is an absolute must.

In fact, it doesn't matter what you do, you need to become a great salesperson. Would you rather be an author, or best-selling author? Would you rather be a struggling musician or have a string of platinum selling records? Even if you are a parent, you are still selling your children on the idea of going to bed or tidying their room!

Businesses of every industry are desperate for great salespeople, but those salespeople must remember one vital factor - they are the face of the company.

Because salespeople are often the only people that interact with customers, this position is one of the most crucial roles to building and maintaining public appearance. Your reputation as a business must be embodied by those that engage with your clients, in both first impressions as well as ongoing relationships. If you suffer a bad initial sales experience, there is a very good chance you will never become a client of that business.

If you walked into a retail outlet and were ignored by the staff, how long would it be before you walked back out of the store? The salespeople probably don't even realise the impact this has on the business, but who is it that complains later when the marketing team are not pulling people in through the doors?

How about a telesales call where the person gets your name wrong right at the start of the call? What about when the call connects but the salesperson clearly isn't expecting the call? The company spends a fortune generating data for their salespeople to call, only for the sales operative to make a mistake, not be prepared, mispronounce a name or generally just fumble the call.

What about the following situation? A woman pulls into a car garage with a flat tyre. She clearly needs a new tyre but the mechanic behind the desk ignores her, then walks off. A few minutes later, someone else comes up to the desk, busy with another task but asks if he can help. His attention is not entirely with the woman, but he gets the point that she needs a new tyre so goes to get the tyre person. A couple of minutes later, the original mechanic shows back up, asking abruptly what she needs. She doesn't exactly know what tyre she needs, so the mechanic begrudgingly wanders over to her car to inspect it. In the end, the woman buys a tyre and drives away. The mechanic thinks he did a great job selling her the tyre, but doesn't realise she will never be returning to that garage again.

First impressions are always vital, but as we have already hinted at, long-term loyalty is where the real value of a customer is realised. Two men, both fathers, haven't been to the dentist for a couple of years and both book a check-up at their local practice. Both require fillings in their teeth and both pay the same for their treatment. A couple of weeks later, both men have a problem with their fillings and they fall out. Dentist A isn't available but the receptionist immediately blames the man for not following the aftercare protocol and suggests he books in for an expensive emergency repair treatment. Dentist B takes the call personally and explains that there are a number of possible reasons, and stays a little late that evening to accommodate a free emergency inspection.

If you consider that scenario, Dentist A makes a little more money in the short term, charging for an emergency appointment and whatever treatments were required. However, when the man gets home, it turns out his kids also need the dentist. How likely do you think he is to book them into the same practice? On the other hand, Dentist B goes out of his way to service his patient at no extra charge. Instead, he is genuinely interested in making sure his client gets what he paid for. When his patient's kids need the dentist, of course he is going to book them in with the same dentist, plus his wife who it turns out needs expensive cosmetic dentistry work doing as well. That example demonstrates the importance of the lifetime value of a customer.

In the new paradigm of sales, the quick win doesn't work in the long term. Quick wins leave a sour taste in the mind of the customer, significantly reducing the chance of them ever doing business with you again. Plus, with social media, their views are no longer just their own.

When was the last time you Googled your name or your business name? What are your clients saying about you? The thoughts and opinions of the world will likely be shaped by their interactions with your salespeople. What sort of example are they setting for you?

The bad news is that there are very few chances to learn the set of skills required to be effective as a salesperson in today's economy. Sales training within businesses tends to focus on product knowledge and positioning rather than creating expert influencers and relationship builders. The businesses tend to teach the same processes that have been successful in the past, or put their top salespeople on pedestals for everyone to copy without giving the full picture of their accomplishments. It also focuses on sales and pipeline management, often of lower importance to the salesperson but useful information for the sales manager who needs to report at the monthly meetings.

There is plenty of information out there in the book stores on how to build strong relationships and use neuro-linguistics to communicate effectively and build rapport. The problem is that most of these ideas either aren't written in a way that connects with salespeople or don't recognise the urgency of sales pipelines and targets and instead focus on creating the idealistic situation of relationships but no persuasion. Also, trainers of neuro-linguistic programming have very rarely, if ever, been anywhere near a sales environment, so although the theories are often sound, there is a disconnect in how to apply these ideas in the real world.

It was this disconnect which became the basis of my training for the next ten years. I needed to find a way to teach the powerful tools of neuro-linguistic programming to sales people in a way that they both understood but could also apply immediately to their sales roles. It needed to be practical enough that it could be taught in a step-by-step method. It also required enough detail and background information so that, once the salesperson had mastered it, they could also then understand why it works so that this same technique could then be used in other situations, not just sales.

I realised that if I could find this combined approach, it would be possible to change the entire image of salespeople. If salespeople were able to combine influence and persuasion with genuine relationship building skills, the customer experience would become one of happiness and excitement, not the dread and apprehension that faces so many consumers today. We would be able to shake off the stereotypical salesperson caricature and make sales a profession such that when you introduced yourself at a party, people would be intrigued, in the way they might be if they met a brain surgeon and wanted to know all about their job.

This new approach to sales would close the gap for salespeople who understood the new approach and customers and prospects who were tired of the old instances and who desperately wanted a new buying experience. These next level salespeople would be able to immediately win business from customers that had started to shop around because of the dissatisfaction with their current supplier relationship. These salespeople would immediately start to develop a following of very loyal customers who would trust any recommendation they made, making these salespeople a much sought after resources in the marketplace.

At the same time, salespeople operating using the old patterns would be left scratching their head at why they had lost so many long term customers. Finding themselves in the pressurised situation of falling behind their targets, they would jump back into the marketplace, hunting down new prospects to close and harass to hit their numbers. This additional time selling would mean those clients that were still loyal would get reduced attention, loosening the bond with the salesperson even further. Plus, the prospects this desperate and pushy salesperson did connect with would become even more convinced that they were looking for a different approach. Frustrated, the salesperson would head back to the office, blaming the quality of the leads before the old-school sales manager turns on the clip of Glengarry Glen Ross and then explains how to 'close' more effectively. Believe me, the successful salespeople of yesterday are the sales managers of today, and this is exactly the message they are communicating.

As a sales trainer, I have frequently frustrated salespeople asking me how to improve their close rate or how to be more effective in dealing with gatekeepers. Sales managers would ask me to make their team more assumptive during the close to give the prospect no way out of the sale. At first, they didn't understand that the old school approach of 'always be closing' was no longer effective, but I still had to deliver this style of training. I had to find a way to teach neuro-linguistics covertly, sneaking the techniques and ideas in 'under cover' disguised as traditional sales methodology.

This is what this book is about. If you read this as a salesperson, you will get lots of techniques and strategies that you can apply immediately to your sales process in a very practical manner. If you read this wanting to understand neuro-linguistic programming, you will see the very models and patterns that are taught in every practitioner and master practitioner course across the world as well as many of the advanced models that are useful for salespeople to understand.

However, I want you to read this book as someone who wants to know how to sell in the new paradigm. The new paradigm does not separate sales from communication. The new paradigm does not say persuade or build relationships. The next level approach combines the two worlds of salesmanship with the integrity and ecology of genuine rapport and relationship skills. If you read this book looking to combine the required skill sets, this is what will make you a master salesperson in the new economy. That is the basis of Next Level Persuasion.

# CHAPTER 2
## HOW NOT TO USE NLP

I was just getting started in training NLP when I was invited along to a sales training course. It was designed for travel reps who were about to head off and spend the ski season at various resorts across the world and their management team, as part of their final meeting, had decided to bring in some NLP experts to give them some tips on how to be more effective at selling the various packages that were on offer. These young people had two appetites: have as much fun as possible at work and earn as much commission as possible. A couple of hundred salespeople filled the dining room of a beautiful hotel and looked on eagerly as the experts were introduced who they hoped were going to help fill their pockets with as much commission as they could carry.

Within about two minutes, the energy had dropped, leaving an atmosphere about as warm as the slopes these salespeople were about to head off to. The trainer was doing a great job teaching, but there was too much of a gap between the knowledge that was being imparted and the practical application of that knowledge, which the salesperson wanted to learn. Believe me, if these salespeople had tapped into the knowledge that was flying around the room, they would have had an incredible snow season and made some serious money. The problem was, I suspect, that the question inside each of their heads was, 'How can I make money immediately?'

I knew from that moment that I was not going to make that mistake. I promised that when it came to my turn to teach, I would ensure that I addressed the needs of the salesperson first. I would find a way to help these salespeople see how important this knowledge was and then give them practical techniques they could apply right from day one.

A few months later I found myself at the front of the room, about to embark on a two-week sales training course. And do you know what I did? I did exactly what I had seen in that hotel room training. I made every mistake that I had told myself I would not make and I saw that exact same look on all of the delegates at my training.

At the end of the first day, I went back to my hotel and tried to figure out how I could rescue the rest of the two weeks I had available. I looked at the content I had planned out and tried to figure out how I could make it more relevant to salespeople. The problem was, what I had designed was NLP training, not sales training. I managed to get through the rest of the course and by the end of the two weeks, the delegates had learned a lot, some of which would even help them turn out to become great salespeople. However, it was a long way from what needed to be taught.

I needed to make some significant changes, not necessarily to the content, but in how this content was communicated. How could I teach NLP concepts that made up the basis of sales techniques in a way that salespeople would connect with, but which allowed me to train using the content I knew would help make the difference?

I also knew I needed to be able to give them real world examples of how to get it right and wrong in a sales scenario. Luckily, I got to attend a lot of sales meetings, both with my trainees and as part of my work, so I could both observe and practice the techniques I was going to be teaching. I even attended sales meetings in countries where I couldn't speak the language, but this allowed me to experiment with the non-verbal elements of communication which I knew to be of massive importance.

It was a steep learning curve, but over time, I eventually developed the techniques and training methods of Next Level Persuasion. The words and phrases that were the basis of my NLP trainings started to disappear, being replaced with a language that salespeople would recognise. I realised that if I wanted to be able to teach the next level of persuasion, I was going to have to start from the inside. If a sales manager wanted training on closing, I would train the heck out of closing skills. However, I made sure that I also covered the bit that came before the close so that I didn't set my trainees up for frustration. I took every opportunity I could to teach what was requested, but also help salespeople understand the context and background to what was being taught.

Eventually, I was able to teach every element of a sales process using sales-friendly language, but in a way that every single aspect of sales had been broken down into a psychological process underpinned by neuro-linguistics. I developed stories for each scenario that seemed like I was going off on a tangent but really allowed me to teach using metaphor. I developed simple-to-understand processes that could be applied by both beginner and advanced salespeople alike to help them improve the results they were getting. I also helped salespeople understand the sticking points in their sales process so that they could access the training that was particularly relevant to them and their success.

Over this time, my students achieved varying levels of success. Two of my trainees were so successful selling that they decided to start their own business and went into partnership with Microsoft. They had gone into IT sales, learned the technical aspects of business, and having built up the required relationships, went on to create a business that better served the needs of their clients.

One student I worked with went from being on the verge of being fired to, within just a few months, being the top salesperson for the region three times in a row and getting national recognition for his work. When we first started working together, this young man knew that he was capable of more and was hungry to learn, and smart too. He was so smart, he picked up everything I taught him immediately and just ran with it. It was like decorating with a one coat paint, it didn't need saying twice.

I also worked with salespeople in different situations other than in the business community. I worked with motivational speakers and international trainers who spoke on stage in front of hundreds, even thousands of people selling their products and services en masse. During this time, I helped shape sales pitches and presentations that sold millions and millions of pounds worth of education. One new speaker that I got to work with had not done a huge amount of this kind of work, so we spent some time together going over the details of his pitch and how he needed to communicate this to the audience. Ninety minutes later, his sales amounted to over half a million US dollars.

These may seem like great results, but some of my favourite feedback has not been related to commission or sales targets. Instead, I love hearing the kind of stories which involve my students attending a training course and then stopping smoking. Or when they go home and use the same techniques that are designed for sales, but because they understand why these processes are effective, use them at home to improve their personal relationships with their partner or their children. This may seem crazy, but by the end of this book, you will understand how someone could learn sales techniques while simultaneously turning their entire life around. Needless to say, this wouldn't happen in any old training course, but mine were designed a little differently, as you now know.

This journey built the foundations and context for Next Level Persuasion. This is far more than just a NLP book written for salespeople. This book will dramatically change your life if you let it. I have built into this book some of the same techniques which form the basis of my live training courses, because I want you to make the kind of lasting change to your sales approach which will pay off in all areas of your life.

I have taken training materials that could easily cover a whole month of training without duplicating content and squeezed them into one book, breaking everything down into easy-to-follow processes and chunks. Study the overall framework to understand everything that goes into Next Level Persuasion and then jump back into each section to fully master the techniques that will make you a next level persuader.

If you read this book once, you will understand what the new paradigm of salesmanship is all about. However, mastering the techniques takes time and practice so don't expect to become perfect after speed reading this book. Instead, read, practice and then revisit the sections which you feel need more attention. If you need to be more effective at starting a conversation, read the section on Opening and pick one or two of the techniques to play with over the next few days. If you feel that you are not generating enough rapport, study some of the techniques in the Connecting section of the book and apply them to your sales presentation. It has taken me over ten years to figure out the important elements of selling, and I know I will continue to learn and practice as long as I am still in sales myself.

# CHAPTER 3
# WHAT IS NEXT LEVEL PERSUASION?

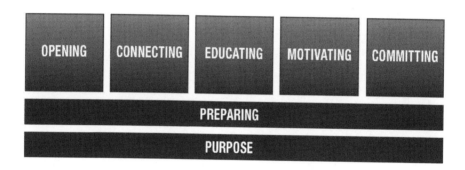

I really should have more patience as a sales trainer, but when I get calls from people that are clearly reading from a script, I can't help but get a little playful. As these calls tend to come from people soliciting products or services that are better left to spam emails (my particular favourites are the computer virus calls or the ones that want to talk about my recent road traffic accident), I don't feel guilty. If you ever want to play, the game is to say the one thing that throws them off their script so completely that they have no idea where to go. You can also play a 'rodeo' version of the game which involves keeping the person on the line for as long as you can until they realise they are not going to get a sale.

What makes me laugh with so many of these sales scripts is how incredibly wrong they can get it. Right from the start, they mispronounce your name or get it wrong completely, which really sets the whole mood of the ensuing conversation. They then begin by asking some obscure questions to try and engage you in the call before quickly moving on to tell you about their product or service. Throw in a little hard sell at the end and then reproduce as many times as possible without an increase in quality.

Now while there is a place for guidelines for salespeople to follow, relying entirely on a script is the sales equivalent of putting together an Ikea wardrobe and calling yourself a carpenter. Sales is more like a game of tennis, with a range of shots that can be played in any sequence. A good serve can put you in control right from the start, but if you always run to play your forehand immediately, how will you ever win a game? Instead, you need to be able to react as the play unfolds in front of you, delivering the appropriate response to whatever your prospect throws at you.

The good news is there are only a handful of shots you really need to master, and these apply to all sales scenarios. If we are going to continue the tennis metaphor, you need to be able to serve at the start of any interaction and then smash the ball home at the end of the point. In between, you have an exchange of forehand and backhand shots which sometimes you control and sometimes your opponent leads. And occasionally, the ball hits the net and you need to be able to react with deftness and dexterity to keep the point going.

These five shot types correlate to the five processes which occur throughout the sales process. Within each of the processes, Next Level Persuasion will provide you with a range of techniques and strategies that will help you to be effective and improve your performance.

Although every sales scenario is different, whether you are selling vacuum cleaners or international software deals, each of these five steps will apply in your overall sales interaction. Sometimes these will all happen over the course of a five minute sale and in other cases, they may happen over a number of different dates and meetings. You may call them by different names, but by the end of this section, you will understand what each of the elements relates to and why it is important to develop this part of your sales skill set.

The process of Opening is how you first contact your prospect and we all know the importance of first impressions. What do you say to get your prospect's undivided attention? Why should this potential client spend time with you and how do you get this information across concisely and with impact? With so many distractions and drains on our attention, how are you going to differentiate yourself from the rest of the noise out there?

Once you have their attention, Connecting allows you to deepen the relationship. In order to convince your prospect to take the actions you want them to take, you need to be able to take control of the conversation and this can only be done once sufficient rapport has been established. Matching and mirroring of body position is not enough for next level persuaders, so understanding how to develop a proper connection with your prospect is essential.

In order to make the right decision, Educating your prospect is an essential process. Your prospect needs to feel fully informed of the entire context so that they feel they are making the right decision. Feeling cornered into making a decision is never healthy for any relationship, and so strategically educating your client is essential so that they feel they are making the right decision which is also in your favour.

Knowing which decision to make and actually making the decision depends on how Motivating you are as a salesperson. You need to learn how to get your prospect excited at the thought of buying from you. This comes down to both knowing the driving factors that determine what decision your prospect will make in any given situation, and also how to link those factors to the product or service you are selling.

The final step of the sale is prospect Committing to the deal. It is the signature on the line, the cheque in the hand or the money in the bank. A deal is never a deal until the prospect has committed by taking action, usually in the form of a financial transaction. You need to facilitate that first step and remove any final obstacles and objections that may exist before the decision can ultimately be made.

Underpinning the sales process is all of the Preparing that you do as a salesperson. Your preparation will help you to get into the right state of mind to enter a sales situation. How well do you know your product? How confident do you feel in your own abilities? What do you know about the person or organisation you are selling to? The more information and understanding you possess before you start to sell, the greater the likelihood of your success.

The last element of Next Level Persuasion is that of Purpose. Although not an element of the overall sales process, there is one factor that all of the top salespeople have in common and that is a strong and definite reason for working as hard as they do. This may be different for every salesperson but there is a clear correlation between a clear purpose and the sales results that are achieved.

Before you think of this book as a paint-by-numbers approach to sales, I want you to understand that sales is both a science and an art. Science allows for formulae, set processes and replication. Art however requires a creative touch which is often unpredictable in nature. Sales should never rely on a script but there are common steps which all sales processes will go through. Although Next Level Persuasion provides an outline and a certain number of linguistic patterns, there is no script. You will need to learn how to incorporate these elements into your sales presentation in a way that is most suitable for your prospects.

If you are a new to sales, I suggest you read through the entire book and then get out into the world and experience as many sales situations as possible. There is no better way to learn about people and sales than to get out there and attempt to sell with a curious and open approach to each interaction. In each sales situation you find yourself in, become aware of some of the techniques and models as they arise naturally and once you notice how they happen by accident, you can start making them happen intentionally. Rather than trying to learn all of these techniques and become a master salesperson immediately, understand that this balance of science and art requires experience. Be in no rush to get to the top.

If you are experienced at selling, read through the whole book then diagnose the areas of your sales process which need focus. Once you know the area to work on, focus your time on developing the understanding of the techniques within that section until it becomes a strength of yours. Whilst I am not a fan of ironing from underneath and making your weaknesses your strengths, you will likely be held back by those parts of your sales process which you do not pay attention to. Don't try to master too many techniques at once, rather pick one or two at a time and stick with them until they become natural, then move onto the next.

Over the years, I have been able to refine my teaching methods to the point where I can convey the appropriate message concisely and precisely, and yet, I have still yet to find a way to teach the techniques so that they are mastered immediately. True mastery comes when you understand the finer points and the subtleties that are involved in any skill, and this only comes through experience. Attempting to master these new skills and techniques in your next multi-million pound deal may therefore not be the most suitable practice arena. Have you ever tried to learn a new language and ended up spitting all over the place as you try and master the new sounds and pronunciations? Well learning these new communication patterns will likely be a similar process, hopefully minus the salivary showers.

The good news is the models and techniques involved within this book apply to so many different forms of communication. Instead of trying these ideas out on your top prospect, instead try influencing your friends or family (especially your kids to get them to do their homework or clean their room) or even complete strangers. Of course, do not try this on your spouse or significant other. If they do find out you are trying to get them to do the things you want them to do, make sure you have mastered the reframing and objection handling chapters first. However, many of the sales people I have trained over the years have reported dramatically improved close personal relationships once they learn these communication skills.

# CHAPTER 4
# PREPARING

| OPENING | CONNECTING | EDUCATING | MOTIVATING | COMMITTING |
|---------|------------|-----------|------------|------------|

**PREPARING**

**PURPOSE**

*"The greatest discovery of my generation is that human beings can alter their lives by altering their attitudes of mind."*

**- William James**

*"A pessimist sees the difficulty in every opportunity; an optimist sees the opportunity in every difficulty."*

**- Winston Churchill**

Woah, hold your horses!

Before you go racing ahead to the sales techniques, strategies and the seven words to overcome ANY objection (yes, that does come later!), it is important to get an understanding of the foundations on which Next Level Persuasion has been built. If you are truly going to become a master communicator and persuader, you have to have the right foundations, otherwise when you apply the techniques that are to come in this book, your complete congruence will not come through.

*It is not the will to win but the will to prepare to win
that makes the difference.*

I have never been a big one for preparing, and I have learned its importance the hard way. If you have ever run a marathon, you will know that you cannot just turn up on the day with a positive mindset and complete the 26.2 mile distance. You need to train for months, putting the miles into the legs so that, come race day, you have built the foundation required to complete (and hopefully enjoy) every step of the course.

Next Level Persuasion is no different. Sure, you could turn up to a sales meeting and apply some of the techniques in this book and they would work. However, that is not my goal for you. Instead, I want you to know why they work and why you should apply the different strategies in each of the various situations. And you can only understand this if you know what Next Level Persuasion was built upon.

Also, you will discover in this book about the idea of 'congruence' which is where the message you are communicating verbally is consistent with the non-verbal signals you are giving off. You may be saying all of the right words, but if you do not have belief and certainty coming through your tonality and body language, the full impact of your message will not come across.

Ok, you are still reading so let's begin our look at preparing. To start with, we will look at the underlying background of Next Level Persuasion which is NLP or Neuro-Linguistic Programming.

# WHAT IS NEURO-LINGUISTIC PROGRAMMING?

*"Neuro-Linguistic Programming is a model of interpersonal communication chiefly concerned with the relationship between successful patterns of behaviour and the subjective experiences (esp. patterns of thought) underlying them", and "a system of alternative therapy based on this which seeks to educate people in self-awareness and effective communication, and to change their patterns of mental and emotional behaviour."*

**- Richard Bandler**


*"There are people who are recognized as being particularly adept in their performance. NLP is the bridge between being jealous of these people and admiring them, it gives a third way, a set of strategies to unconsciously assimilate precisely the differences that make the difference between this genius and an average performer. It is an accelerated learning strategy, a mapping of tacit to explicit knowledge, a program that allows you to explore one extreme of human behaviour – namely excellence."*

**- John Grinder**


I was first introduced to NLP when a good friend of mine handed me a CD program by someone called Anthony Robbins. At the time, I had no idea who this was, but my friend thought that some of the techniques he taught might help me in my personal training business. He was right. Even after studying the very basics of NLP, I found that I could create lasting change with my clients rather than have to shout at them to run around a field. I was hooked. I had to learn more.

Over the years, I studied with a number of different training schools, all of which brought something a little different to the table. However, wherever you learn NLP, it is important to why it was developed and how it has grown over time. Let's have a quick fly along the timeline that is the history of NLP.

In the 1970's, Richard Bandler and John Grinder postulated a connection between a person's neurology, their linguistics and the resultant behaviour.

---

The pair observed the work of therapists Virginia Satir, Milton Erickson and Fritz Perls and attempted to codify the methods each used in their therapy sessions. These modelling sessions allowed Bandler and Grinder to put together a language, methodology and set of techniques that, in theory, would allow anyone to recreate the results that these therapists had spent years refining.

Once they had developed certain models that would allow them to recreate therapeutic processes, the pair started sharing and experimenting with the results they could create. Word spread, and soon the likes of Robert Dilts, Judith DeLozier and Leslie Cameron became involved, helping to develop the concepts even further. Other contributors included Michael Hall, Steve and Connirae Andreas and David Gordon. Each of these individuals brought something new to NLP, building continually on the initial concepts of Bandler and Grinder.

Fast forward a few years and as the technology and practice of NLP developed, so did the idealogical gap between Bandler and Grinder as to how to do NLP 'right'. As the founders of NLP argued over who owned what, many of those involved in the development of NLP went on to train others in its use and application. Soon a number of organisations began offering practitioner and master practitioner courses, each branded with their own unique approach towards NLP. As the number of people using NLP grew, so did the diversity within the application of the technology.

One development that helped bring NLP out of the therapy world and into the awareness of the masses was the transition from the psychiatrists couch into the personal development world. NLP was rebranded as a way of helping everyone to create the results they wanted in life. If you wanted to be more successful, you needed to learn NLP.

This brings us back to Anthony Robbins. After studying with John Grinder, Tony Robbins took NLP to the masses by repackaging the tools into seminars and audio programs that allowed individuals to set and achieve goals and get greater results in life. As I mentioned, it was one of his audio programs that got me started on my journey. He has continued to teach many of the tools of NLP in his seminars for over 30 years, although he has developed these techniques further and rebranded his technology as Neuro-Associative Conditioning.

(If you get the chance to see Tony in action, I highly recommend it!)

That pretty much brings us to the NLP that exists today. Although it still exists in the therapy world, it has taken a bit of a bashing as a pseudo-science and is generally considered to be unreliable when applied in a therapeutic setting. Treatments such as CBT (cognitive behavioural therapy) are now preferred.

Instead, NLP is now positioned as holding the secret to quick and lasting change and is used by motivational speakers, life coaches, authors and trainers all over the world. The techniques that exist within the toolbox of NLP really do allow people to either make changes in their lives by helping them to create empowering visions for the future and, at the same time, letting go of the limiting beliefs that hold them back.

NLP has also proved popular in the corporate world. With so many different possible applications for the concepts and models within business, there has been a surge in books and training courses available to employees, managers and executives at every level of the organisation. Employees can learn how to communicate with customers for either sales or service. Managers can get an understanding of how to manage staff and get the best possible results from their team. Executives can model the greatest leaders and orators from history to help get their vision across to the entire organisation.

Today, there are so many different ways to learn more about NLP and its applications. You can improve your knowledge to the practitioner and master practitioner levels and there are advanced trainings that help you develop this understanding for situation specific uses.

Did Bandler and Grinder think when they began developing NLP that the technology and methodologies would spread so far and end up impacting so many people? Now that NLP has grown beyond them both, it will be interesting to see what the future holds in terms of developing new techniques, models and application.

So now you know more about the history and development, let's look at the fundamental building blocks that make up NLP - The 3 Pillars.

---

# 3 PILLARS OF NLP

If Next Level Persuasion is built on a foundation of Preparing and Purpose, the basis of NLP is that of the three pillars. You actually already know these three pillars and practice their application every single day without knowing it. In fact, everything in NLP happens naturally, but NLP helps us break down the complex processes we go through in our psychology to give us a way of replicating the most effective patterns.

Think about your journey to work in the morning. You wake up, get dressed and head out the door with a very definite goal or destination of arriving at work. You jump in the car/hop on the train/climb on your bike/mount your horse and begin your journey. As the minutes go by, you see signs to your destination and the distance is decreasing which means you are heading in the right direction... well done! However, today there is a diversion and your normal route is impassible. What do you do next? Well, you might take a different road in your car or change from the train to a bus for the last bit of your journey. Ultimately, you know where you want to get to and you are prepared to do whatever it takes until you get there. In the end, no matter what obstacles arise, you arrive at the office.

Well that one process involves all of the secrets to success in every area of life, not just sales, and this is what makes up the three pillars. You need to decide upon your goal or Outcome, the end result that you want from all of your efforts. You need to have the awareness or Acuity to notice if you are moving in the right direction or not. Finally, you need the Flexibility to be able to change your course if the circumstances require it. These are the three pillars, so let's explore them a little further.

## OUTCOMES

*"If you don't know where you are going, you'll end up some place else."*

**- Yogi Berra**

*"Never leave the site of a goal without first taking some form of positive action towards its attainment."*

**- Tony Robbins**

The first pillar of NLP is that of setting an outcome. The process of setting goals has been around for thousands of years. We can trace goal setting back to the ancient Greeks who had a word Telos, which mean 'end' or 'purpose'. Processes or actions that were teleological were taken in search of that outcome.

In NLP, outcomes are the starting point of all activity. Once your outcome has been set (and we'll explore how to set PURPLE outcomes later in the book), you have created the target for all your subsequent actions. A goal or outcome without action will never materialise, and so whenever you set a goal, it is vital to take action. However, you need to ensure that the activity you are engaging in is taking you in the direction of your goal.

## ACUITY

*"The difference between something good and something great is attention to detail."*

**- Charles R. Swindoll**

*"The first step toward change is awareness. The second step is acceptance."*

**- Nathaniel Branden**

Acuity is an acuteness of vision or perception, particularly towards the finest of details. Having a well developed sensory acuity allows you to be aware of subtle changes in things such as colour, sound, or the way someone moves? With regards to your outcomes, it is the ability to notice whether the actions you are taking are being effective and moving you towards your goal or not.

For example, you are in a sales meeting, going over some of the key features of your product when your prospect suddenly shifts posture and changes their tone. Do you notice this change, or do you blindly carry on talking about your product? Every sales person needs to develop this ability, and if you are currently losing deals without knowing why, then this skill will make a huge impact on your results.

## FLEXIBILITY

*"When one does something that reaches a bad result, then one does it again several times, expecting a better result - is one not a crazy monkey?"*

**- Voltaire**

*"It is not the strongest of the species that survives, nor the most intelligent that survives. It is the one that is the most adaptable to change."*

**- Charles Darwin**

Assuming you have the acuity to notice what does and doesn't work, the final pillar of Flexibility allows you to change your behaviour when something isn't working. The Law of Requisite Variety, a concept from Cybernetics, dictates that the person with the most flexibility in any given situation will control the situation.

In sales, this can be demonstrated in the ability to hold a sales conversation without a script whilst having the acuity to notice if what you are saying is being effective. Take the example above of your prospect shifting in their seat: what do you do next? The amateur sales person will continue with their set course, but the sales professional will know how to alter their conversation to get the desired reaction in this situation.

To develop flexibility in your sales behaviour, there will be a number of different techniques for each situation in this book. There are also hundreds of other sales books with their own perspective on how to be effective in a given situation. Identify the areas you want more flexibility in, and then commit to learning the ways that will allow you to control those situations rather than continually being at the effect of your prospects.

As mentioned, this approach to life guarantees success as long as you maintain focus on your outcome, acuity to notice if your results are moving you in the right direction and the flexibility to change your behaviour if required. When you start to incorporate Next Level Persuasion into your sales processes, I want you to keep these three pillars in your mind.

Perhaps you are going to try using the neurological levels questioning model and really want to get your prospect using a metaphor to describe his or her desired situation (this will become clearer later). This is your goal. You then use your acuity to notice how much rapport you have developed and when a suitable moment arises to ask the appropriate question. Finally, when your prospect doesn't quite understand the question, you have the flexibility to be able to rephrase the question to get the desired result.

Maybe you have picked out a particular prospect and really want to have them as a customer of yours. Well you have a clear outcome, so now you need to take action. Normally cold calling works for you, but for some reason, this prospect does not take sales calls. So what do you do? Do you keep calling hoping eventually to get through? Well, maybe you can try different times of day but your acuity tells you that isn't going to work. So instead, you start attending networking events and trade-shows that you know this prospect also attends. You start sending brochures in the mail, or emailing industry updates to them in your newsletter. You have the flexibility other sales people do not have, and this is what will make you successful when it comes to winning this new customer.

## PRESUPPOSITIONS

If you are going to communicate with congruence and integrity, it is vital that the thoughts going on in the back of your mind do not conflict with the words that are coming out of your mouth. As you will discover later, the belief in what you are saying communicates far more information than the words themselves, so developing a strong set of supporting beliefs is a way to generate significant improvements in your selling ability even before we move onto the linguistic techniques.

When using NLP in a therapeutic setting, the necessity to change lies with the client as they are coming to you looking to stop smoking or to improve their self esteem. However, in sales, the salesperson often needs to create this desire in their prospect. With this in mind, the beliefs of a salesperson need to be focussed around having control of a situation and acting in a way that supports and motivates the prospect. Knowing this, the presuppositions of NLP become even more important for a salesperson to not just understand, but to embody.

The presuppositions act as a guiding philosophy and mindset that helps form the foundation of NLP. Each of these beliefs has been created to help empower you as a salesperson, supporting you to deliver effective messages and decode the information given to you by your prospects. (As you will find out later in this book, beliefs are simply statements that we have decided to adopt as the truth.)

These presuppositions, therefore, are neither true nor false, and in many cases could be argued either way. However, should you adopt the positive, empowering aspects of each of these statements into your own belief systems, you will find that this helps you become a more powerful influencer and communicator.

As you read through the presuppositions, I want you to think about what each means to you. Some of the statements may seem a little abstract to begin with. However, take the time to uncover the meanings and, more importantly, how you might be able to apply these lessons in your sales situations. I have given you a couple of insights into how they might be interpreted, although I am sure you will also be able to add to these yourself.

## THE MEANING OF COMMUNICATION IS THE RESPONSE YOU GET

Have you ever asked a child if they have the time and they turn around to you and simply say 'Yes'? Now although this may seem like a trivial matter, how many times do you know of requests that have been communicated that have been actioned differently? As salespeople, it is our responsibility to control the sales process, and this includes the actions you want your prospect or customer to take. We often need to be more specific than we think. For example, take the word 'regularly' which indicates a particular frequency of occurrence. Now I like to think that I run 'regularly', maybe once or twice a week. Now I have a friend who also runs 'regularly', every 3rd of February, regular as clockwork. Although we often use the same words, their meanings can be very different to each of us. If you find that you are not getting the response you want, look at how you are communicating your message. How can you be flexible and change your approach to get your desired outcome? Do not expect the customer to change for you. Instead, become a chameleon of communication, able to fit the needs of your client.

## YOU CANNOT NOT COMMUNICATE

Albert Mehrabian's widely quoted findings on communication state that only 7% of communication actually comes through the words we say. So many sales people spend time writing out scripts or opening statements that are designed to have impact, but then when it comes down to the delivery, they miss the mark. This is because the rest of the message is delivered through tonality (38%) and body language (55%). It is not necessarily the facts which are being miscommunicated, rather the emotion and fortitude of belief which accompanies the message. Congruence, the alignment of your message and how you say it, is a huge contributor to trust, and all sales people know the importance of trust in making a deal. Think about how you communicate, not just what. If you do not believe what you say, there will be incongruence. If you are nervous in a meeting, there will be incongruence. If you have not done your preparation and research, there will be incongruence, and your prospect will pick up on it, either consciously or unconsciously. Ensure you are fully aligned and congruent with your message for every sales call.

## THE MAP IS NOT THE TERRITORY

Even the best map does not have all of the information about a particular place. Rather, maps are useful summaries of a location that contain key elements such as places of interest, transport links and maybe where you can eat or shop. However, look up from any map and you will see details and information that no map could ever contain. This is the same when you are talking with a prospect. Because we filter the information we take in, process it internally and then have to recall it when asked a question, a lot of the accurate details can get lost in translation. When communicating, a good sales person will search for the information beyond the initial response if necessary.

## PEOPLE MAKE THE BEST CHOICE AVAILABLE AT A GIVEN TIME

You have two jobs to do as a sales person. You need to motivate your prospect to make a decision and you also need to educate them to make the right decision (meaning your product or service). Assuming you have done the motivation part, your prospect will then make the decision to go with the solution that best suits his or her needs. Part of your pitch needs to be educating the prospect about what a good solution looks like. How can they make the best decision for them or their business? What are the most important factors to consider when looking at finding a supplier or your service? Know your product's unique strengths and then educate your prospect towards making a decision that takes these elements into account.

## EVERY BEHAVIOUR HAS A POSITIVE INTENT

I remember a particular sales person who was never deterred by getting rejections over the phone, or getting knocked back by gatekeepers. His reaction was to put the phone down, curse in some way for a second, then pick the phone straight back up and make his next call. Now although this may appear to be a good sales trait, not taking rejection personally, his reaction to the person rejecting him forgets this presupposition. Instead of blaming the other person and getting momentarily angry with them, perhaps he should have explored the reasons behind the rejection a little more fully. Where was the benefit in the gatekeeper rejecting him, not to him but to the gatekeeper? What did rejecting him mean there was more time to accomplish? Once you take this viewpoint, working with gatekeepers becomes less of a challenge. In fact, I challenge you to one day call a number of organisations and just speak to the gatekeepers. Don't try and sell them anything, just try and understand what it is like to be in their position. Gatekeepers can take over 300 calls in a day, so no wonder they try and get rid of you as quickly as possible. Instead, think what you can do to make your call beneficial, and allow the gatekeeper to change their behaviour to supporting you instead.

## NO SUCH THING AS FAILURE ONLY FEEDBACK

If you only hear yes as a salesperson, you aren't asking enough. Human tendency is to play a little safe and avoid experiencing rejection, or failure.

Instead, we need to learn to embrace these opportunities as chances to grow. The feedback that comes through getting something wrong will help us develop our sales skills. In this book, you will be presented with a number of new ideas, and you will need to let go of your previous sales strategies in order to adopt them and see how they work for you. Like rebuilding a golf technique will take you back a few strokes before you improve, you may find that using some of the techniques in this book will feel a little unnatural to begin with. However, stick with them, learn from each experience, and before you know it, you will have developed new proficiencies in selling and communicating.

## MIND AND BODY ARE CONNECTED

Sales people need to be able to communicate to both parts of the human system as decisions are made using both the mind and body. The body is the emotional side of thought, which is truly how we make our decisions. We are guided by our feelings, making statements such as 'it just felt right' or 'I had a bad feeling about it' when we are forced to make a choice. It's not always something we can describe with any accuracy, more of a sense we get. However, we then try and justify our decisions logically, which uses our mind. If we choose to do something, our explanations tend to follow the word 'because', such as 'I bought the new television because we needed a new one and it was a great deal'. If we choose not to do something, we often use the word 'besides', such as 'I didn't buy any advertising this time, besides we are getting plenty of referral business right now'. Sales people that tend to rely solely on the logical sale will find themselves hearing maybe a lot as they don't hit the motivation of the prospect. Sales people that only use emotional selling techniques will experience a lot of buyers remorse and returns once the excitement has worn off.

## THE PERSON WITH THE MOST FLEXIBILITY IN A SITUATION WILL CONTROL THE SITUATION

*"Notice that the stiffest tree is most easily cracked, while the bamboo or willow survives by bending with the wind."*

**- Bruce Lee**

Have you ever had a phone call from a telesales organisation that employs people to read from scripts in an attempt to sell to you? They prattle on for far too long and then ask you a question in an attempt to engage you in the conversation (I know this seems like a sweeping generalisation, and I admit it is, but it is also a warning to those of you that use the phone to sell!). The challenge to see if you have a sales person on the end of the phone rather than just a reader is to throw something into the conversation that doesn't fit the script. Refuse to answer a question, throw in a random fact, tell them what the weather is like or ask them about their holiday; anything that will throw them off course. If they struggle, flap and go quiet, they aren't a real sales person. Sales people engage in conversation and that, as we all know, could go anywhere. It would be like playing tennis and getting upset when someone plays it to your backhand when you were expecting a forehand. You need to have the flexibility as a sales person to handle any element. Do your preparation so you know your product in detail. Research your prospect and prepare in advance the questions that you may be asked. Practice asking the same questions in different way in case your prospect doesn't give you the answer you are looking for. Any time you find yourself in a situation that you cannot handle on the spot, ensure that you immediately go and seek out 5 different ways to handle that situation next time. Commit to developing the flexibility of behaviour and you will be able to handle any sales situation that arises.

## POSSIBLE IN THE WORLD, POSSIBLE FOR ME

I want you to challenge yourself as a sales person. Look at some of the greatest sales people on the planet, such a Joe Girard. Joe has been repeatedly recognised by the Guinness Book of World Records as the greatest sales person on Earth, and worked in used car sales, a notoriously tough industry. However, someone has to be the best, so why not Joe. If you survey sales people in most industries, you will find the Pareto principle in effect. 20% of the sales people will earn 80% of the commissions. Do those in the top 20% work harder and more hours than the rest? Not necessarily, in fact, probably not. Instead, they tend to do lots of little things a little bit better. Your challenge is to develop yourself to become the best sales person you can be, maybe even the top in your industry. Focus on doing the things that are in your control, rather than sales figures that are often controlled by your prospects. Work on your communication skills, make the most sales calls, phone the prospects that others are afraid to. Put the effort in up front and great results will surely be the effect. Someone has to be the best sales person in your company or industry, so why shouldn't it be you? Simply commit to learning the skills of those top sales people and then go one little step further.

## IF YOU KEEP DOING WHAT YOU'VE DONE, YOU'LL KEEP GETTING WHAT YOU HAVE GOT

In this book, I am going to encourage you to attempt new sales strategies in order to improve the results you are getting. Some of these may feel easier than others, but all will have a positive impact on your ability to communicate with your prospects and clients. In order to improve the results you are currently getting, you must do something different. Albert Einstein once said "No problem can be solved from the same level of consciousness that created it". In order to develop yourself as a salesperson, you need to raise your level of awareness (learn something) and then put this new knowledge into action (do something). When you try out these new techniques, I encourage you to be playful and curious with their application.

## SEEK FIRST TO UNDERSTAND, THEN BE UNDERSTOOD - COVEY

This quote from Stephen Covey should be every sales person's mantra. I have been in countless sales meetings where the prospect asks one question early on, and then the sales person decides it is time to talk non-stop about their product or service down to every last little detail. When this monologue is finally concluded, the sales person is greeted by an astonished face of someone that has just absorbed far too much information in far too short a time. The result is rarely, if ever, in favour of the sales person. Instead, the goal should be not to talk about everything your product has to offer, rather just the bits that are relevant to your prospect. To do this, you need to understand the person in front of you; their challenges, their goals, their outcomes. Spend time uncovering this information in detail and by the time it comes to pitching your product, you will be far closer to hitting the mark.

## AN OBJECT IN MOTION STAYS IN MOTION UNLESS A FORCE ACTS AGAINST IT - NEWTON'S FIRST LAW OF MOTION

Sir Isaac Newton probably wasn't thinking about sales when he came up with his theory, but this concept is important for all sales people. The worst word for a sales person is 'maybe', which is only ever heard when the sales person has not applied enough force to get the prospect to take action. The force I am talking about here is that of Motivation. Sales people need to be expert motivators as well as influencers. You need to understand what makes someone tick, what gets them off their backside and take the action you want them to take. We will cover the concepts of motivation in this book, and why both the carrot and the stick (this will become evident later) are useful at different times. Apply enough drive and motivation and your prospect will take action. Your job as a sales person is then to steer that motivation in the correct direction (your product ideally!).

## PURPLE OUTCOMES

The first pillar of NLP is Outcomes, and so everything we do needs to start with setting clearly defined goals. A goal focuses our attention and stops us getting pulled off track by - oh, look, a shiny thing! My point exactly. As you will shortly discover, our brain is actually designed to chase goals by ignoring all the distractions and focussing only on those things that support your achievement and success. Without goals, we are making things harder for ourselves. With goals, we know our unconscious mind is working overtime in our favour.

As a salesperson, it is vital to have goals for every area of your performance, including the outcome of a sales meeting. However, many people set ineffectual goals if they set any goals at all. We have probably all heard of SMART goals (specific, measurable, achievable, realistic, time-bound) but this system is designed more for management than success. Instead, we want to structure our goals in a way that gets the power of our unconscious mind proactively working for us rather than sitting idly in the background with nothing to do.

**NEXT LEVEL PERSUASION**

So how do we do that? NLP has the well-formed outcomes which help put a positive structure around any goal setting process. To create well-formed outcomes, they must be PURPLE!

**P**ositive

**U**nder Your Control

**R**oute

**P**roof

**L**ogistics

**E**cology

## P - POSITIVE

Since the mind is not able to process a negative, all goals must be stated in the positive. Anyone who has tried NOT to eat chocolate for example will know the torture of knowing that your emergency ration is there in your cupboard, waiting for you to have a momentary lapse in will power before it pounces. Consider the alternative, which is to think about the healthy food you want to consume, or the exercise you want to do instead.

As a sales person, you will have obvious sales targets and goals that are nearly always positive. However, think about your other goals. Not wanting to be bottom of the sales leaderboard is not a good way to think about things. Instead, focus on the position you want to be and hold that image in your mind instead.

Keeping your goal in your mind activates the Reticular Activating System (RAS), the part of your brain that recognises and draws attention to important information.

For example, when you last bought a car, you probably didn't see many people driving that particular model. However, as soon as you drove out of the showroom, immediately everyone else had bought the same car. How was this possible? Well, those cars were always there, you just didn't have your reticular activating system programmed to look for those cars.

Framing your goals in the positive will help program your reticular activating system to be on the lookout for opportunities to help you achieve your goals.

 **I want to make the most calls this quarter!**

 **I don't want to be in last place again!**

## U - UNDER YOUR CONTROL

If you set a goal that is reliant on someone else, then you may find yourself frustrated if they do not go along with your plans. For example, you want to be promoted but the boss chooses someone else. You want to sell a deal to a prospect but she decides to buy from another supplier.

The way to solve this frustration is to frame your goal in a way that is 100% within your control. For example, instead of trying to get promoted, your goal should be to ensure that you have taken all of the necessary training courses that someone in that role would need to have completed. Instead of selling the deal, set the goal of delivering the most powerful sales presentation you have ever given.

By setting a process goal rather than an outcome goal, you will give yourself a far greater chance of feeling successful. You will also avoid the frustration of not being in control of your outcomes.

 **I want to make contact with 100 good prospects this month!**

 **I'm going to make a sale in the next 2 hours!**

## R - ROUTE

When I played American Football, we used to have a visual tree of routes (pronounced 'rowtz') that would tell you here a particular player would be on a given play. Knowing how you are going to get to your goal and the potential obstacles, defenders and challenges you are going to face will make it a lot easier than just running around aimlessly hoping you are going to reach your destination.

For example, imagine using a satellite navigation system without putting in your start and end point. How could it ever calculate a route for you?

As a sales person, you are going to be embarking on a journey. Along the way, there will be key milestones and stepping stones that you need to identify before you set off. By knowing these journey markers, it helps you to know that you are on track and making good progress.

 I know if I do my lead generation my target is in sight!

 Trust me boss, this month it's in the bag!

## P - PROOF

The proof of the pudding is in the eating and the proof of a goal is your end step. Proof is the evidence you expect to see, hear or feel when you arrive at your destination. If you are unclear in what you want your outcome to be, how will you know that you have arrived?

What do you need to see or experience to believe that you have arrived at your outcome? Where will you be? What will you be doing? How will you be celebrating?

One easy bit of proof for a salesperson lies in their commission cheque at the end of the month. That little piece of paper can be all the evidence you need to know that you have done the job you intended to do, and that you are now being rewarded appropriately.

 When I hit my goal I will have the commission cheque in front of me!

 I'll just keep my head down and I know I'll get it!

## L - LOGISTICS

Rarely do you undertake a journey to the magnitude of your goals without a little assistance along the way. What resources do you need to help you on your journey? What is going to help make the journey easier? Faster? More enjoyable?

Logistics can include tangible items or products that may physically make your life easier. Logistics can also include ideas such as knowledge and training or people and your network. For example, getting extra knowledge on a particular aspect of your product may help you sell it more effectively. Having a manager that leads and inspires you to be your best can help accelerate the journey.

Decide on the resources and logistics you need at the various steps along your journey and then plan accordingly.

 **I'm going to use my coach/manager and listen to audio tapes daily!**

 **I'll figure it out as I go along!**

## E - ECOLOGY

You have to be sure your goal is worthwhile and holistic, both to you as well as those you interact with. For example, you may have a goal of earning £100k per month, but if you need to work 18 hours a day, how will that impact your health and relationships? When you set your goals, think about the wider reaching implications, not just the direct result of their achievement.

 **I will hit my targets and maintain my work/life balance!**

 **If I stay awake all week and just sleep all day Sunday, I can do it!**

# STATE MANAGEMENT

*His palms are sweaty, knees weak, arms are heavy*

*There's vomit on his sweater already, mom's spagetti*

*He's nervous, but on the surface he looks calm and ready*

Eminem rapped about the importance of state management in 'Lose Yourself' when he talked about choking on stage and not being able to get the right words out. This is the extreme of what can happen when you allow your nerves to take over you, but most sales people have experienced something like this where we find ourselves in a great situation but panicking about what to say.

Managing your emotional state can be a difficult job for sales people. You have to maintain your calm when approaching the end of a really big sale and not look too excited. You have to regain your motivation when a prospect rejects you and tells you to get lost on a phone call. And no matter what happens at the end of the month, you have to do it all again tomorrow!

Sales really is a roller coaster ride. I have seen sales people skipping around the office giving people high-fives one day and then slumped over their desk the very next day. As exciting as this can be, it can also be exhausting. Come the end of month, tension and stress rise as the deadline for hitting targets get closer and this can be where sales people appear desperate to get a deal.

I nearly always find that the top sales people in any organisation tend to stay more emotionally consistent. Yes, they celebrate good deals, but are keen to get back on with their work towards the next sale. Also, if they hit a roadblock, they also seem to bounce back quickly. This consistency allows them to produce the results they do as they avoid the negative implications of letting their mood drop.

You might think that if the top performers are always in a good mood and the poor performers struggle to maintain their positivity that emotional states are dictated by your sales results. However, in every sales organisation, there are also people that go against this rule. I'm sure you know a top sales person

---

that is always grumpy, or one who is struggling slightly, but always remains positive.

The truth is that results do not dictate your mood. However, they can play a part if you let them. The reality is that you are in 100% control of your emotional state at all times, and once I share with you the formula, you will easily be able to create any emotion you want.

**Luckily, the formula is just the combination of 3 different factors:**

- Physiology
- Focus
- Internal Dialogue

## PHYSIOLOGY

This is the combination of all of the elements of how you are using your body right now, and is probably the biggest contributor to your mindset right now. Stop for a moment and think about what kind of mood you are in, and now think about how your body mirrors that.

For example, if you are a little stressed, perhaps you are a little hunched over, you probably aren't breathing very deeply, and your muscles likely feel a little tight, especially across the back of your shoulders.

However, if you are feeling unstoppable, the chances are you have your shoulders back and chest pushed out, you are breathing deeply and controlled and instead of tight, you are feeling strong throughout, especially in your core.

Your physiology has a direct impact on your mood, so think about how you use this as a sales person. Get frustrated and stressed making calls when you are sat down with your ear holding the phone to your shoulder? Try standing up instead (this is one of my favourite tips for any salesperson using the phone) and get a handsfree headset that allows you to gesture and move freely.

---

**NEXT LEVEL PERSUASION**

## FOCUS

How you are focusing the lens of your mind will determine the way you interpret any given situation. For example, you come in early one morning to try and catch people before their working day, but instead of getting some early success, instead you are faced with endless answer machines and phones that just ring ad infinitum. What is your focus after that point?

The phrase 'bad things happen in 3s' is akin to this idea. If you wake up and stub your toe as you get out of bed, you may start to look for the other two things that are destined to be coming your way. However, if you train yourself to look for the positive then you will maintain a very healthy attitude and mental state.

Remember how the reticular activating system works? Maintain a positive focus and you will see even more reasons to be positive. Being positive is contagious, but so is being negative. Take control of your focus and learn how to see the opportunity in every situation.

## INTERNAL DIALOGUE

What you say to yourself will play a huge part in how you feel. The problem that a lot of people have, however, is that they tend to be better at putting themselves down than building themselves up. (Sales managers and sales targets don't always help matters either so beware!)

There are two types of internal dialogue challenges that you need to be aware of and then actively try to correct if you notice yourself acting this way.

## PERSONAL STATEMENTS

How do you talk about yourself? Do you say to yourself 'I can't cold call' or 'I'm not very good face-to-face'? Do you put a limit on yourself by believing in glass ceilings that others may have told you about?

Affirmations are really useful in these situations, and I encourage all sales people to surround themselves with posters, post-it notes and other such

---

ornaments that reinforce positive messages of self belief. Change the screen saver and desktop image on your computer. Listen to motivational audio programs between meetings and on your way into the office. Refuse to indulge in gossip and rumour mongering when in the office (especially if it is about you!).

Repeat positive phrases to yourself every day and you will soon change the way you talk about yourself. You will notice one of two things happen. Either you will begin talking positively about yourself, or (even more fun) you will argue with your internal dialogue. This happens as it goes into auto pilot, telling you how rubbish you are, and then your new, positive internal voice jumps in and shouts 'No I'm not! Actually, I'm pretty awesome!'.

(And for those of you wondering what internal voices, those are the ones I am talking about!)

## WHY QUESTIONS

Have you ever asked yourself a question about why something happened? Chances are you ended up with a whole range of answers from the sensible to the absurd to the down right crazy. The trouble with 'why' questions is that they tend to send you on a loop, looking for as many possible explanations about the situation at hand. Not terribly useful.

Instead, start to ask yourself a better quality of question. Do you really want to know the reason behind something, or would you rather figure out what to do with the information you have before you. Instead of asking 'why does this always happen to me?', instead ask 'what can I do to massively improve my situation?'.

If you can direct your questions to give you more empowering answers, you will find yourself in far greater control of your emotional state.

## WHICH STATES DO I WANT?

As a sales person, which emotional states do you want to embody? Try and figure out what you would need to do with your physiology, focus and internal dialogue if you wanted to experience the following emotions:

| | | |
|---|---|---|
| Confident | Powerful | Assertive |
| Understanding | Thoughtful | Curious |
| Passionate | Empathetic | Driven |

## ANCHORS

Your brain has a natural tendency of linking things together as a way of establishing a cause-effect relationship. These neuro-associations are how we learn what works and what doesn't.

For example, when we are younger, we want to fiddle with everything. One day, we pick up something hot and we burn ourselves. Our brain immediately links the pain with whatever we just picked up. This linkage allows us to avoid experiencing that same pain again in the future.

Anything that is unique and happening at the same time at the experience is likely to get linked up, especially if the experience is intense enough. If the emotion or sensation is not as powerful, you may create a neuro-association if your brain gets multiple examples that are consistent over time.

Your brain is constantly creating neuro-associations, and once you figure out what these are and how you can create them yourself, you can use them to your advantage.

In NLP, we call these neuro-associations anchors, and they are usually related to emotions. When these anchors are 'fired', we are able to re-experience the emotion that is linked to the action.

For example, think of a song that reminds you of a particular person and which leads you to feel a certain way. In this case the song is a trigger for you, as your brain has anchored a physiological response or emotion to the song. If you suddenly change the context of the relationship with that person, you will get a different reaction when you trigger that anchor. Remember that song that reminds you of your first girlfriend/boyfriend? It probably started off bringing happy thoughts, but then you broke up and it made you sad, and now... well I guess that all depends doesn't it?

It is possible to create anchors by getting into a particular state or emotion and then doing something unique at the peak of the emotion. Common anchors involve kinaesthetic moves ranging from a unique way of touching your knuckles through to punching the sky.

However, for sales people, I suggest you begin with taking advantage of pre-existing anchors.

I recommend using musical anchors, especially now that we are able to take our music everywhere with us on our phones rather than clumpy Walkmans. Listen to a song that gets you into the right mindset before a sales meeting and you will notice the difference. Not only will they put you in a great mood, the right song can fill you with energy and some even have lyrics that will empower you and make you feel unstoppable (anything from the Rocky soundtrack will do the trick here!).

Music is used in a very calculated way in retail shops to put you in the buying mood. Listen next time you are in a department store to what music is playing in each section. What mood do you think the store is trying to get you into by using that specific piece of music. Think about airports as well. They create a soundscape of peace and tranquility in an effort to distract you from the tension and anxiety caused by queueing for the security checks. Music can be used to help generate all sorts of emotional shifts. Just try watching a scary movie with the sound off and see if you get the same internal reactions.

As you now understand, state management is something that you control and that you can directly influence. You don't get motivated or frustrated, but rather you 'do' motivation or frustration through the unique combination of your physiology, focus and internal dialogue that leads to that outcome. Want to feel better? Change one of these three elements, or fire an anchor in the form of a piece of music that gets you in the right state and frame of mind for the upcoming sales situation.

## BELIEFS AND MINDSET OF A SUCCESSFUL SALESPERSON

If you watch the start line of the Olympic 100m final, you can probably tell who is going to win before the starter fires his pistol. There is an air of confidence about the soon-to-be-champion that sets him or her apart from the competition. If this is true for the worlds' best, just think how big this difference would be with the average athlete.

Of course, physical ability plays a part in athletics, but what really sets the best apart from the rest is their mindset, their mentality and beliefs about themselves and their ability to compete. To be a successful salesperson takes a similar winning mindset, a set of values that drive you ever forward in search of that next deal and beliefs that keep you moving in the right direction.

In fact, to be successful in sales takes the same commitment and dedication as it does to win an Olympic medal or win a Nobel prize. There are common traits in all successful individuals, and here is my core list on what makes someone stand out from the crowd.

## A CLEAR DECISION

Mohammed Ali is well known for his phrase "I am the greatest!", but did you know that he used to say this well before defeating Sonny Liston to win the world heavyweight boxing championship? Ali had made up his mind and committed to becoming the best boxer the world had ever seen, and it was this decision that was the first step towards his achievements.

The greatest salespeople in any company are those that are committed to becoming the best. They have decided that they will be the best and will do whatever it takes to make that happen. If you can imagine the effort and intensity that Ali put into his training, then you will recognise this focus in these individuals. There is a hunger inside of them and, like Rocky, they have the eye of the tiger.

If you want to be the best, you need to decide to be the best, and you must be prepared to do whatever it takes to get there.

## A STRONG WHY

*"He who has a strong enough why can bear almost any how!"*

**- Friedrich Nietzsche**

To be a huge success, you are going to have to overcome obstacles and, from time to time, these are going to be a serious challenge. Many people would look at these insurmountable hurdles and give up. Successful people however realise that what is on the other side of the hurdle is far more worthwhile than the effort it will take to get there.

If you have a big enough reason why, you will do whatever it takes to be successful. Why are you a salesperson? By the end of this book you will have a deep understanding of values and how they motivate, but ask yourself now, why have you chosen sales as a career?

Is it because you want ultimate control over your finances? Do you want to be able to provide for your family and those around you? Are you the kind of person that needs to be around people every day? Do you want to know that you are making a difference by helping people solve their problems?

When times get tough (and they will!) you need to remember WHY you have chosen this career. Re-associate to this and you will find your motivation never wanes.


## CLEAR GOALS

Sales targets are set by the business for the business. If you work for someone else then your revenue targets are set in order to help the business reach its financial projections. If you work for yourself, perhaps you have set sales targets that realistically fit in with your business plan. Whatever the case, your sales goals will always be realistic, but will they be enough to give you what you want?

Driven sales people always know their numbers and how much commission they are going to earn. They can also tell you exactly how they plan to spend that commission when it comes in. The top in the field have good taste and high standards, and this is part of what drives them every single day.

What do you want to be able to buy? A house? A car? A holiday? What are you working towards? Make it something bigger than you have ever expected for yourself. Raise your standards and you will love the energy you find to make things happen.

Set yourself clear goals, not just for how you plan to spend your commission, but also for your development too. Sales is a great vehicle that helps you get somewhere, but you need to know where you are going. Want to move into management? Want to set up your own business? Stay focused and keep your goals with you at all times.

## RESILIENCE

It's not nice when someone puts the phone down on you, or tells you to get out of their office, or swears at you, or suggests that you put your samples into places samples shouldn't go! We have all met people like that, and the chances are, you have probably done something similar to people who have tried to sell to you too.

Great sales people don't take things like that personally. They find a way to justify the other person's actions. Perhaps it was a bad day, their cat had just been run over, someone had bought decaf coffee instead of the real thing, or they were in the bathroom when the toilet paper ran out! It doesn't matter what the situation was for the other person, a great sales person always remains in control of their next actions.

You need to have resilience. Put the phone down, laugh it off, and then dial again immediately. Get right back on that horse. If you get kicked out of someone's office, go straight to their competitor and tell them what happened and that you want the opportunity to "repay their kindness". Whatever happens, don't let it knock you from your path.

# PERSISTENCE

*"The gem cannot be polished without friction, nor man perfected without trials."*

**- Chinese Proverb**

A no is not always a no. Sales people realise that persistence is the key to unlocking some of the most valuable opportunities that are out there. However, rather than just take the same action over and over, great sales people combine persistence with creativity to think of other ways to get the same result.

A good friend of mine found his biggest client in a takeaway food restaurant. In fact, this client was the biggest client in the world for the entire business, and he found him by buying a chicken burger. How? Well, he was clear on what he wanted, which was to work with a particular business, and he repeatedly approached the business trying to find out who was in charge and to arrange a meeting. However, he was stonewalled every time.

One day, after getting another no, he decides to get something to eat at the restaurant next door, and asks the guy behind the bar whether he knows the owner of the business. The guy replies no and then takes my friends order. Then he asks my friend why he is looking for him. My friend responds with a small summary of what he did, and the guy behind the counter starts arguing with him. "You can't do that, that's impossible!". My friend just wants to eat his food, but keeps talking with the guy and the conversation gets progressively more and more intense.

Eventually, the guy behind the counter tells my friend to finish his food and then follow him (apparently the chicken shop attendant was a big guy so he didn't say no!). They walk out of the shop, into the business next door, and out towards the back of the offices. My friend gets excited, thinking he is about to be introduced to someone in the business. The man opens the door to the office, walks behind the desk, and then introduces himself as the owner of the business. The rest is, as they say, history.

Figure out who you want to sell to, and then don't give up until you have the meeting with that person. Do whatever it takes to get yourself in front of that prospect and then do an incredible job when you get there.

## PERSONAL DEVELOPMENT

I have been in the personal development seminar world for years and have seen so many different ways that these ideas can be used. However, I don't think there is any occupation on earth that requires you to put these lessons into practice as often as sales does.

Sales is a career which is constantly testing your mindset, requires you to be a masterful communicator, understand people better than they understand themselves, be a motivator, help people overcome their fears and concerns and break through to new results. In fact, having trained life coaches and motivational speakers, the job description of a salesperson is not so different.

You need to get as much self improvement and personal development information into your daily routine as possible. The more you can learn in these areas, the more successful you will be, I can assure you.

Below are a few of my personal recommendations if you have not read them already:

- *Think And Grow Rich* - Napoleon Hill

- *How To Win Friends And Influence People* - Dale Carnegie

- *The Seven Habits Of Highly Effective People* - Stephen Covey

- *Personal Power* - Anthony Robbins

- *Who Moved My Cheese* - Spencer Johnson

- *The Secret* - Rhonda Byrne

- *Go Givers Sell More* - Bob Burg & John David Mann

- *Influence* - Robert Cialdini

- *The Master Key To Riches* - Napoleon Hill

- *Feel The Fear And Do It Anyway* - Susan Jeffers

These books have all had a significant impact on my life, so I suggest you get a few of these, but then continue to read and explore your own path of learning.

Don't have much time to read? Get these as audio books instead and listen to them in your car, on the train, in the gym, whenever you have some time in between meetings. Think of what you listen to as feeding your brain. Do you want to listen to music, which has no nutritional value, or would your rather feed your mind and imagination with new ideas and techniques that will help you become an even more powerful salesperson and communicator?

I have to mention TED before the end of this section. TED is a non-profit devoted to ideas worth spreading in the areas of Technology, Entertainment and Design. They bring together some of the most incredible, inspirational and innovating speakers on the planet for their conferences and then share these talks on their website. They also have an app for your phone, so you can download videos and talks and listen to them as you are going through your daily routine. The ideas in some of these videos are truly incredible and come directly from leaders in business and science. Make sure you visit TED.com today and download their app too.

> *"We are what we repeatedly do. Excellence, then, is not an act, but a habit."*
>
> **- Aristotle**

Can you see now why Preparing is so important? What you do before you pick up the phone or get to your sales meeting has such an impact on your results that it would be crazy not to pay attention to this stage of the process. As Benjamin Franklin once said 'An investment in knowledge always pays the best interest' and your investment in preparing yourself will continue to reward you throughout your sales career.

**Here are some of the main points to take away from this chapter.**

- The secret to success lies in the three pillars. If you know what you want and take action in its direction then notice what works and change what doesn't, you are guaranteed success, not just in sales, but in all areas of life.

- Adopt the attitude and methodology from the presuppositions of NLP as the basis for your positive sales mindset. As Ralph Waldo Emerson put it, 'What you do speaks so loudly that I cannot hear what you say', so ensure you always believe in yourself and your message.

- Get clear on your goals and outcomes and remind yourself of them often. Have a clear pathway in mind that guides your most important activities each day so that you are constantly making progress. Then develop the resilience and persistence necessary to last the journey.

- Commit to continually improving yourself. As a salesperson, the better you understand people, the more effective you can be at influencing and persuading so as well as learning sales techniques, become an avid student of the human mind.

# CHAPTER 5
## OPENING

| OPENING | CONNECTING | EDUCATING | MOTIVATING | COMMITTING |
|---------|-----------|-----------|-----------|-----------|

| PREPARING |
|-----------|

| PURPOSE |
|---------|

*"Think twice before you speak, because your words and influence will plant the seed of either success or failure in the mind of another."*

**- Napoleon Hill**

*"Success depends upon previous preparation, and without such preparation there is sure to be failure."*

**- Confucius**

Research suggests that during the first 7 seconds people will make assumptions about us. We call this our first impression, and making a good one is vital for sales people. Unfortunately, we are playing a but of an uphill battle from the start with the typical preconceptions of sales people. Therefore, doing what we can right from the start to make a good first impression will help.

In football, new players (rookies) are told that if they ever find themselves in the endzone, act like they have been there before. (This saying was developed after the embarrassment that ensued from poorly prepared end-zone celebrations following touchdowns.)

In sales, you need to act like you have been there before. You need to be prepared. The start of the meeting sets the tone for how your entire business relationship is going to pan out.

In tennis, there is an advantage to the person who serves, and this rings true in sales as well. You can control the beginning of the interaction and doing a good job here starts you and your prospect on the right foot.

However, in tennis, your opponent hits the ball back to you, and they too are trying to win the point. If you serve and then run to play a forehand but your opponents hits the ball to your backhand, you will lose the point.

Similarly in sales. If you are restricted by your sales process and your prospect wants to take the conversation along a different line, you will likely lose rapport.

In this section, we will look at how to start a sales meeting with impact, giving yourself the best possible first impression and getting your prospect immediately onto your way of thinking. After this section, you will have to develop your behavioural flexibility to deal with any situation that may then arise.

# INTRODUCING YOURSELF

As a sales person, you have a lot of roles to play during a meeting. You have to be the rapport builder, the educator, the motivator, the persuader and the convincer. You need to take your prospect through an emotional journey from positive during the early stages, to negative where you try to discover the motivating factors that will drive the decision, back to positive as you talk about your solution. In order to do this, you really need your prospect to be listening to you from the start.

Problem!
Your prospect has questions... in their head... which they will not ask.

Without writing a follow up book called 'mind reading for sales people', I can actually tell you what these questions are. In fact, most prospects will have the same 3 questions that, once you have answered will allow them to give you their undivided attention. The good news is they are not terribly difficult. Those questions are:

> Who are you?
> What do you want?
> Can I trust you?

If you answer each of these questions then you can proceed with the meeting. If not, they will continue to be at the front of your prospect's mind and as you are there giving your best ever presentation, they are still there thinking about their questions and not paying any attention to you at all.

Have you ever met someone that you know but have forgotten their name? They start talking to you but you aren't really listening, you are just desperately trying to think of how you know them, where you met them and anything that will just give you a reminder of their name. Then they ask you a question and all you can reply is 'huh?'. That is the level of distraction you can expect your prospect to exhibit if you do not answer these questions in advance.

## QUESTION 1 - WHO ARE YOU?

How do you introduce yourself? Do you lead with your job title? Do you lead with your name? Do you lead with your history?

The deeper query behind this question is why are YOU the person I should be listening to? With this in mind, you need to be able to give a strong personal story that explains to your prospect the value of listening to you in this meeting. Do not rely on the strength of your product offering alone, but instead identify what you bring that is unique in this situation.

If you work for yourself, you may find that your business and individual pitches are similar. If you are an employee then you need to tell your prospect what makes you unique versus the other salespeople that work alongside you.

## QUESTION 2 - WHAT DO YOU WANT?

By stating at the start of the meeting what you want to cover, this will allow your prospect to relax as they know what to expect. You might tell them that you are going to start with a little information about you or your company, then move on to understanding more about their current situation and desired goals before finally exploring the possibility of working together.

ALWAYS mention the last element of working together. Your goal should be to have a smooth running sales meeting. If you do not tell your prospect, then there is likely to be an uncomfortable apprehension as they wait for you to try and sell to them. If you have told them upfront that there will be a pitch then they will relax and recognise it when it happens.

You can even send over an agenda ahead of the meeting if this is suitable for your style of selling. This can help reinforce your appearance as a professional sales person rather than someone who just wants to take their money.

During this element, you should also hint at the benefits of working with you or your product. What are the statistics or qualities that make you stand out from your competition? What is in it for your prospect if they chose to work with you? Don't go into detail, but start to dangle that big carrot in front of them and grab their attention with an exciting fact or statistic about your results.

## QUESTION 3 - CAN I TRUST YOU?

This is often referred to as your credibility statement. You have just made a statement about the results you can offer and now you need to back it up! Credibility and trust can be exhibited in a number of ways.

Testimonials, or social proof, are a great way of getting people to believe that the results you are offering are possible. If no-one else has ever achieved those results then I am going to be a little sceptical about your claim. However, if you have hundreds of satisfied customers then I want to know about them, especially if they started in a similar situation to me. Be prepared to talk about some case studies or examples early in the meeting to help your prospect develop that element of trust.

Recognition by authority is another way of showing credibility. If you have won the award for best XYZ in your industry then this demonstrates excellence. Perhaps you were recognised by the government, or the local chamber of commerce, or by the PTA at your child's school. Try and develop recognition for yourself and your business and then use this as a great credibility tool.

Association to excellence is a key to developing trust. Let's say you are a partner of the biggest company in an industry, this will help you appear more trustworthy. Perhaps your client portfolio is packed with high profile names? If so, drop a few of these into conversation and you will see the look of excitement and belief on your prospect's face. By borrowing credibility from others you are associated with, you can make yourself more believable.

## PRE-FRAMING THE SALES MEETING

*"Tell them what you are going to tell them*
*Tell them*
*Tell them what you told them."*

**- Aristotle**

Later on in this book, you will discover pre-framing as a way of handling objections before they arise during a sales meeting. However, we also want to use the concept of pre-framing right at the very start of your meeting in order to set the expectations of your prospect and also give yourself the best chance for closing towards the end.

Literally, pre-framing is setting the frame or context of the interaction before anything takes place.

In sales, pre-framing involves letting your prospect know, upfront, what is going to happen during the sales meeting. We do this so that your client can relax, safe in the knowledge there are going to be no surprises. You are setting the scene for the meeting, telling them what is going to happen, what they can expect from the interaction and giving them an idea about how the meeting will start, develop and end.

Part of pre-framing a meeting is setting the agenda. Not only does it give your prospect a feeling of security (it looks like you have done this before), but it also allows them to understand what is going to be happening during the time you are together. You do not have to give a full breakdown of everything that is going to happen, rather an overview, a preview of this meeting's coming attractions (just don't do the cinema fanfare impersonation!).

> *"Ok Miss Smith, here is how I think we should proceed today. To start with, I really want to get to know your situation in more detail, so let's start by you telling me more about where you are currently and where you see yourself heading. We can then look at some of the challenges you are currently facing in terms of achieving those goals. Then, at the end, if I think there is a way my product might be able to help you, we can have a look at what it is I do. How does that sound? Is there anything else in particular you want to cover?"*

This is how I would suggest you set out a verbal agenda at the start of your meeting. Depending on the context, you can make it more or less formal, but in a 1-to-1 situation, this relaxed introduction works well.

## 1 - Understand Your Client's Current Situation

Always start with understanding your prospect's situation in more detail (you won't be able to sell to them effectively if you do not know this in detail). You want to find out where they are and how they got to this point.

## 2 - Understand Your Client's Desired Situation

Preframe that you want to talk about their goals and ambitions. You want to know the direction that they want to go in. During the sales process, this will allow you to open a gap which hopefully will need your product to close.

## 3 - Discuss What You Can Offer

When it comes to talking about your product, notice that we will only discuss our product if there is a way we can help? This will help your prospect relax, knowing that the hard sell is not going to happen and that you will only try and pitch to them if you think you can add some value. Of course, your job during the meeting is to highlight the gaps that your product or service can help to bridge.

## 4 - Any Other Business

Finally, invite your prospect to add to the agenda. Your prospect may have something specific they want to discuss with you, so allow them the opportunity to add this right at the start. If they do have something to add, this will massively increase their engagement level right from the outset.

Setting an effective agenda at the beginning of your meeting helps you to preframe what is going to happen during the rest of your time together. If suitable, it may even be worth sending this agenda over to your prospect ahead of the meeting. Doing this serves several purposes:

- Immediately set you apart from other sales people they may be meeting in your field;

- Reinforces the sales meeting and helps to reduce cancellation or no-show occurrences;

- Positions you as someone that values both your time and that of your prospect.

Practice your meeting opening and how you will set an agenda. How can you make this structure fit you, your product and your sales process?

## THE 4-MAT

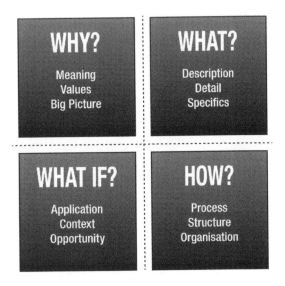

The 4-Mat model by Bernice McCarthy that be used to help understand the questions that go on inside a prospect's head, especially at the beginning of a sales call. As a sales person, you need to understand these questions and answer them, where possible, in advance, otherwise you risk the prospect not engaging with you fully.

As a rule, in any given context, we all tend to have a preference for asking one particular type of 4-mat question. This will be our primary driver as to how engaged we are in a sales conversation. However, we tend to move through a series of questions, proceeding once each question has been answered with the required amount of information.

Addressing each of these questions and in the correct sequence will get maximal engagement from your prospect and keep their attention right through to your product pitch.

## THE 4-MAT QUESTIONS AND SEQUENCE ARE:

### Why?

If your customer's preference is for 'Why' questions, they will tend to be personally involved in the situation and will be looking for the meaning behind the engagement. Your prospect may operate at a higher level and will be interested in the idea and concept.

### What?

'What' preference people need to know facts and want to understand more about the details of your proposal. Your prospect will want clarity around exactly what your product or service is and will need to be able to understand how this will fit into their current situation.

### How?

'How' is about process and practicality. What needs to happen in order for your solution to be effective? What is the first step and the last step? Your prospect may need real life examples before they understand how it all fits together.

### What If?

The 'What If's' tend to be more creative and want to understand what happens beyond the obvious benefits of your product or service. Your prospect will seek to uncover hidden possibilities and applications of what you have to offer, over and above what you have told them.

# 4-MAT ELEVATOR PITCH

Although this model can be used in many forms of communication, my favourite sales application for this model is in creating your elevator pitch. Your elevator pitch is that opportunity where you have only a few moments to capture the attention of a potential prospect and you want them to be intrigued enough to suggest continuing the conversation at a more appropriate time (rather than having to be in a Wall St elevator which is how this type of brief pitch got its name).

In order to do this, you need to make a statement that answers each of the questions above in the prospect's mind. They need to know Why your product or service exists, What specifically it is and how it is positioned in the marketplace, How it works and can be applied to their situation and What If it works, the associated implications that will result.

Below are a few examples for three different products; a time management package for employees, a beauty therapy training school and a franchise business opportunity. Once you have seen a few examples, then you will use the structure to create your own elevator pitch.

## WHY?

(Ask a rhetorical question that will allow your prospect to understand the reason why they would need your product or service.)

- Have you noticed how there are just some people that are always able to remain calm, no matter how busy things seem to be? Aren't they always the people that get the most done too? Wouldn't it be great your employees were those kind of people?

- Have you ever wondered how you can save money on your beauty therapy treatments whilst still maintaining the standard of your appearance? I mean, going to the salon is great, but sometimes you have more important things to do with that time, right?

- Have you ever been frustrated working for someone else and wanted to start a business of your own but don't know where to start? Perhaps you are looking to create a second income outside of work to improve your financial situation long term?

## WHAT?

(Give a description of your product that allows your prospect to know what it is without being able to assume to know everything about you.)

- Well, we have developed our time management product with the latest combination of live training, virtual assistance and practical materials that are tailored specifically for your business.

- At BTS, our beauty training courses are especially designed for people that are looking to take control of their own make up situation and do it for themselves.

- For many people, a franchise is a simple way to start their own business, regardless of experience or expertise, and our franchise is the fastest growing and most established business in the XYZ industry.

## HOW?

(This is a brief description on how your solution would be implemented and what the steps may be to proceed.)

- Your employees will read a module, join a live online workshop and then have work-based activities that will help the concepts become reality.

- You can study during the day, evenings or weekends and we have a range of both full and part time courses that are conducted by highly qualified professional beauticians.

- From the moment you join, we support you with everything from marketing and promoting your business through to managing the accounts and stock control at your premises.

## WHAT IF?

(Let your prospect know the end goal of your solution and the values it meets. What is the bigger picture of working with you?)

- Just think how much more productive your employees can be, freeing them up to engage in some of the projects that they have been keen to do but not had the time available.

- Imagine how great it will feel to get lots of compliments for your professional make up, knowing that you did it yourself and saved a fortune at the same time.

- Finally, the ability to work for yourself growing a business which will either continue to give you a salary or provide you with a valuable asset which may later be sold.

Let's see how those elevator pitches sound when you pull together all of the separate elements.

## TIME MANAGEMENT

Have you noticed how there are just some people that are always able to remain calm, no matter how busy things seem to be? Aren't they always the people that get the most done too? Wouldn't it be great your employees were those kind of people? Well, we have developed our time management product with the latest combination of live training, virtual assistance and practical materials that are tailored specifically for your business. Your employees will read a module, join a live online workshop and then have work-based activities that will help the concepts become reality. Just think how much more productive your employees can be, freeing them up to engage in some of the projects that they have been keen to do, but not had the time available.

## BEAUTY TRAINING SCHOOL

Have you ever wondered how you can save money on your beauty therapy treatments whilst still maintaining the standard of your appearance? I mean, going to the salon is great, but sometimes you have more important things to do with that time, right? At BTS, our beauty training courses are especially designed for people that are looking to take control of their own make up situation and do it for themselves. You can study during the day, evenings or weekends and we have a range of both full and part time courses that are conducted by highly qualified professional beauticians. Imagine how great it will feel to get lots of compliments for your professional make up, knowing that you did it yourself and saved a fortune at the same time.

## FRANCHISE BUSINESS OPPORTUNITY

Have you ever been frustrated working for someone else and wanted to start a business of your own but don't know where to start? Perhaps you are looking to create a second income outside of work to improve your financial situation long term? For many people, a franchise is a simple way to start their own business, regardless of experience or expertise, and our franchise is the fastest growing and most established business in the XYZ industry. From the moment you join, we support you with everything from marketing and promoting your business through to managing the accounts and stock control at your premises. Finally, the ability to work for yourself growing a business which will either continue to give you a salary or provide you with a valuable asset which may later be sold.

**TOP TIPS** - You want to be 'artfully vague' with your description of 'What you do?'. Prospects have a habit of jumping to conclusions if you give them too much information and will jump at the opportunity of pigeon-holing you into a box. It is easier not to get into the box in the first place than to get out of this box once your prospect has judged you and what you offer. However, if you don't tell them enough detail about what you do, they will not be able to associate and make the decision if they are interested enough. Therefore, give your 'what' elements enough information to generate interest but not too much to allow assumptions.

**Note** - I am a big fan of infomercials (you know, those 30 minute long TV adverts for abdominal crunch machines and other such products). Did you know they use this very process to structure their product pitches? Well now you do. And now that you know that, I want you to **AVOID** sounding like an infomercial! Use the 4-Mat model as a framework rather than a script. These examples, when you put them together from the individual elements, could sound quite cheesy. Sometimes the questions are ridiculously obvious and can sound patronising ("Have you ever had a birthday or know someone that has?"), so find a way to make your questions a little more insightful.

## FINISHING AN ELEVATOR PITCH DIRECTLY OR INDIRECTLY

The goal of an elevator pitch is to induce positive reciprocity. This is a complicated way of saying that you want them to say something which lets you know whether they are interested or not.

Directly - If you are talking with a potential prospect, you should finish with a question like "how does something like that sound to you?" or "can you see how this would be useful to you?". Both of these questions are directed at the individual in question and are designed to determine how your prospect feels about what you have told them so far.

Indirectly - If you are at a networking event or similar, the chances are that the person in front of you is not a potential prospect, but someone you are meeting for the first time. DO NOT PITCH THIS PERSON DIRECTLY! There is a good chance that this individual does not need your solution and an even better chance that he or she will know someone that will. If you pitch directly to them and they are not interested, you have lost both the relationship as well as the chance for referrals. However, if you ask a question such as "Do you know someone who might find this useful?", you open yourself up to this individual's entire network. AND, if the person in question is interested themselves, they will of course let you know.

There are so many different ways you can answer each of these question, even for the same product or service. Use the space below to plan your elevator pitch.

## 4-MAT QUESTIONS - WHY? WHAT? HOW? WHAT IF?

Other potential applications for this model include structuring a cold call introduction (which would naturally be similar to the elevator pitch), developing the flow for a sales presentation as well as building a training or education piece for your prospect. However, the applications are endless.

# COLD CALLING

If your job involves cold calling then I applaud you. This has to be one of the most challenging aspects of sales as you have to be a master of two skills. Firstly, you have to be a master of Concise Communication, and secondly you have to be a master of your Emotions.

Concise Communication is about delivering a potentially complex message as simply as possible in as few words as possible. When that person picks up the phone, you literally have a few short seconds to grab their attention and get them to stay on the phone and listen to the rest of what you have to say. Know what you are going to say before you start the call, and make sure you practice your opening lines so that they sound slick but not scripted.

Being a master of your Emotions is critical because you will experience rejection after rejection when you cold call. Trust me, I've been there, and it's not fun. I have even been cold called and put the phone down on sales people before. The important thing to remember when cold calling is that the rejection is NEVER personal! There are a million reasons why people may not want to talk to you that you will never get to hear about once they have put down the phone. Your job is simply to smile, redial, and do it all over again.

Remember the keys to effective state management:

Physiology. Focus. Internal Dialogue.

## MASSIVE - IMMEDIATE - PAIN

The key to concise communication is in getting across the key aspects of your product or service in a way that makes them pay attention to you immediately. Remember that people are driven by three factors: massive effect, immediate impact, or the avoidance of pain. Be sure to include one or more of these aspects in the opening elements of your call.

## NLP TECHNIQUE - PATTERN INTERRUPT

One extremely useful technique for cold calling is the Pattern Interrupt. Used in NLP to break people's state and get them to change the way they are thinking and behaving, pattern interrupts allow you to change the flow of a conversation in the direction you want to take things.

I once did an exercise with a group of sales people and got them to survey the gatekeepers of prospects they had not been able to properly connect with yet. One of the interesting statistics to come from the exercise was that gatekeepers can get up to 300 calls PER DAY. This means that in many cases, the gatekeeper is going to be on autopilot, in a trance designed to get you off the phone as quickly as possible.

Pattern interrupts are great at getting people out of their trance, and if done well, over to your way of thinking. This technique is also extremely quick and simple to do. In fact, any time that there is a deviation from the expected course of behaviour, this is a pattern interrupt.

The classic pattern interrupt example is Milton Erickson's hypnotic handshake induction which allowed him to induce trance almost immediately. This pattern involved him reaching out as if to shake hands but then interrupting the flow of the handshake by grabbing the wrist instead. By continuing this motion of unexpected actions, Erickson was able to induce non-verbal trances and hence begin his therapy work.

When cold calling, we need to think of ways that we can interrupt the expected flow of conversation and engage with the person for long enough to get the rest of our important message across. Here are seven examples of pattern interrupts that can be used when cold calling.

## SAY SOMETHING CONTROVERSIAL

*"Hi there, I am just calling you because I noticed the way you are running your advertising is the exact opposite of the successful people in your industry and I thought I'd call to find out why!"*

By using a controversial statement, you are immediately standing yourself out from the crowd. The vast majority of sales people will use a generic opening line of some kind that makes them instantly recognisable (trust me, I have listened to thousands of recorded sales calls) and easy to bounce. By saying something controversial, you engage your prospects attention as they will either disagree with you and engage in debate (allowing you to put explain your opinion) or agree with you (allowing for further conversation). Either way, the conversation has started.

## MIND READ

*"I know what you are thinking, another useless call about to waste thirty seconds of your life. But, what if..."* and then you insert your unique selling point. Mind reading is a great way to build rapport if you do it well. Pace, pace and lead is how NLP teaches rapport, and pacing is about adopting the other person's model of the world for a moment. There are even inductions which are done using just mindreads and hypnotic suggestions. By mindreading the other person's situation, you can immediately engage in rapport, allowing you to get further into the conversation.

## ASK FOR THE NAME

One of the simplest ways that salespeople can engage, especially with gatekeepers, is to ask for the person's name. All too often, we jump straight into the pitch without finding out who we are speaking with. During the gatekeeper survey that I conducted, we asked what criteria the gatekeeper used for bouncing calls, and general politeness was very high on the list. If you ask for a person's name and can make them smile while you have them on the phone, you have a great chance of having a good conversation.

## GET IT ALL WRONG

I call this the 'bumbling idiot' sales call approach, and I find it can work wonders. In the movie *The Matrix*, there is a scene where Agent Smith explains to Neo that the machines tried to create the impression of a perfect human world and that it did not work. Instead, they created one with problems and imperfections that the human mind associated with more. When you are selling, especially if you are selling to consumers rather than businesses, appearing less-than-perfect often comes across better than the super-slick pitch. We tend to trust this person more, and if someone is terrible, we often want to help them improve and do well. Saying 'good morning' in the afternoon is an easy starter. Try and build in a few small mistakes and see how you get on.

## ASK FOR HELP

There is something inside of us that finds it very difficult to say no when we are asked for help. When you ask someone for help, there is a very good chance they will listen to your story and your request. This will at least give you the time to explain the reason for your call, and hopefully get the other person on your side and helping you to be successful in the call. Get the person's name and then tell them openly you need their help.

## STOP HAVING FUN

If you make a call and the person picks up the phone laughing, this is when you can use this pattern interrupt. Rather than jumping straight into what you were about to say, use whatever is happening in their background to engage in a conversation. In hypnosis, this is called utilisation, bringing whatever is happening in the environment into the induction. Listen right from the start and use whatever happens on the call to engage in a conversation.

## IF YOU WERE ME

*"I'm looking to get onto your approved suppliers list. If you were me, what would you do?"* Open the call by telling the person you are calling what you want to have happen and then try handing over control of the call. This can be especially useful in complex sales situations where you don't necessarily know who you need to speak to or what the internal processes are. People usually expect salespeople to be pushy and take control, so flip this around and see what happens.

Becoming excellent at the Opening stage requires you to put yourself in your prospect's situation and get inside their mind. Remember, most salespeople just want to talk about themselves and their products, so when your prospect encounters someone who seems to genuinely understand his or her needs, all of a sudden you change from being an interruption to being someone they feel they need to be talking with.

**Here are some of the main points to take away from this chapter.**

- Become a mindreader and even before you pick up the phone, try to understand the problems and challenges your prospect is facing. If you were them, what message would you really want to hear from a salesperson? Now, use that understanding to shape your opening statements.

- Set an agenda and pre-frame your sales interactions. By telling your prospect what to expect, it allows them to relax, open up and truly take in what you are saying. If you a planning to sell them something, it is better to avoid the massive shock when you ask them for their money.

- Understand the four standard questions that go on inside all of our minds and use this to help you create you elevator pitch. You want to give enough information that people understand, but leave enough out so that you spark the appropriate interest. Just try to avoid sounding like an infomercial!

- Remember, gatekeepers can get in the region of 300 calls per day so if you sound generic, you are going to be dialling more than you are speaking. Grab the attention of the person on the other end of the phone with a pattern interrupt and then continue to add value during the call.

# CHAPTER 6
# CONNECTING

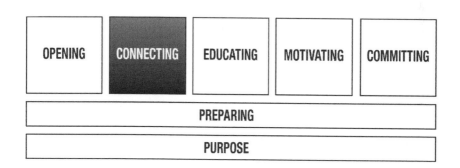

"The way a team plays as a whole determines its success. You may have the greatest bunch of individual stars in the world, but if they don't play together, the club won't be worth a dime."

**- Babe Ruth**

"Don't walk behind me; I may not lead. Don't walk in front of me; I may not follow. Just walk beside me and be my friend."

**- Albert Camus**

*Would you buy from a complete stranger?*

*What about from your best friend?*

The answer to the first question is probably no and the answer to the second question is likely yes. For most of us, there needs to be an element of trust and connection present before we agree to part with our hard earned cash. We are taught from a young age not to trust strangers so we will be hesitant to take what this person has to say at face value without evaluating it somewhat. However, we assume our best friend, with whom we have been through so much (and likely has enough dirt on you to land you in some serious trouble) has our best interests at heart and therefore would not want to deceive us in any way.

Therefore, there exists in our mind some form of continuum of trust and connection we have with people and we classify the people that we know at various points along that line, the complete stranger at one extreme and our best friend at the other. With this in mind, there must exist a tipping point along this continuum where we shift from saying no to saying yes. The tipping point is usually lower for items with less of an emotional attachment and higher for those with a greater level of cathexis or at a more significant price point.

If we know this as salespeople, what do we need to do to move ourselves along this continuum with our prospect until we get to a point where they trust us enough to take our advice and decide to buy from us?

The answer lies in how good we are at Connecting with our prospects.

Our level of connection is made up of a number of factors which we will discuss throughout this chapter and can be developed to such a deep level that you have more than just a salesperson-client relationship with those who you work with. You don't need to develop this further level of connection in order to sell, but I suggest that over time you will want to continue connecting with your clients.

So let's begin our look at connecting by discussing a work that al sales people talk about but which very few really understand.

# RAPPORT

> **Rapport** - *a close and harmonious relationship in which the people or groups concerned understand each other's feelings or ideas and communicate well.*

Every sales person knows of the concept of rapport. This idea of finding 'common ground' and matching body language has been taught to sales people from the very first sales training course ever taught.

However, as we discuss rapport during this section of the book, you are going to realise that these two techniques only scratch the surface of superficial rapport.

Instead, you are going to discover how rapport is really built from a NLP standpoint so that you truly understand the level of connection you are looking to develop. You have to learn the fundamentals first. As we go through this chapter, you will find a number of advanced techniques that allow you to create massive levels of rapport with absolutely anyone.

Warning - when you get good at these techniques, you will literally be able to develop rapport with anyone you meet. Please use with ecology.

## PACING AND LEADING

In NLP, there are two elements of rapport - Pacing and Leading. Pacing is the skill of getting into rapport, and Leading is maintaining rapport whilst taking control of the situation. In his book, *The Seven Habits of Highly Effective People*, Stephen Covey's fifth habit is 'Seek first to understand, then be understood' which summarises the concept of rapport brilliantly.

There are two main mistakes that sales people make when considering rapport:

- Not generating enough rapport;

- Not using the rapport gained to lead the conversation.

I have seen so many sales people go straight into a sales pitch without trying to get to understand their prospects situation and goals. The prospect may ask an opening question, and this is the cue to jump straight into every detail of their product or service.

The other end of the scale is the sales person who is good at getting into rapport but then does not do anything to risk losing that. They don't ask any challenging questions. They are reluctant to ask for the business in case the prospect says no and rejects them.

The goal should instead be to get into rapport and then lead the conversation in the direction you want to take it.

To begin to develop rapport and 'pace' your prospect, you need to be aware of three primary aspects of communication. The famous study conducted by Albert Mehrabian discovered that, during a face-to-face conversation, the element of trust was conveyed in the following proportions:

**55% Physiology**

**38% Tonality**

**7% Words**

This means that the vast majority of your communication has absolutely nothing to do with what you are saying!

This is great news for sales people. It means that you can start to develop rapport before you even open your mouth (I know this is tough for many sales people out there!)

Let's explore these three aspects of communication now and how they can be used to develop rapport.

## PHYSIOLOGY

Most people will have heard of matching and mirroring body language to gain rapport. Adopting the same postures and using similar gestures will often help people feel comfortable with you, and allow you to develop rapport more easily. When thinking about body language, you should consider the following aspects.

## Body Posture

Is your prospect sat up or slouched? Sat forward or relaxed back? Are they tense or relaxed? Is their head position upright or relaxed and slightly to the side? Your ability to notice the subtle movements of your prospect will determine how easy it is for you to adopt a similar body position.

## Hand Gestures

The way someone gestures often externalises the way they process information in their head. For example, someone counting out a list will often point out that list with the side of their hand. If you use similar gestures, your prospect will be very inclined to understand your key points.

## Facial Expressions

Your prospect's face will give you a lot of non-verbal cues into how they are receiving the messages you are communicating. Make sure you are keeping an eye on your prospects face as you are talking, and make a note of the expressions and the possible implications of these.

## Breathing

By getting into rapport with someone's breathing, you can develop a great level of rapport, even to the point of being able to read minds (it's true, I've seen it happen!). Look at the shoulders and notice how quickly they rise and fall (avoid looking at the chest, especially with female prospects) and then adjust your own breathing rate appropriately.

## Eye Movements

Have you ever met with someone who either can't make eye contact or makes too much eye contact? Maintaining an appropriate level of eye contact is about noticing your prospects natural breaks in eye contact, not just staring. It is important to know your own tendencies in this situation.

## TONALITY

The sound quality of your voice plays an important part in developing rapport. It is easy to overlook this important element, relying on natural vocal qualities, but in reality, it takes work to develop a range in the tonality of your voice. This is largely down to us using the same voice every day and never needing to change it. However, sales people will likely find themselves naturally adopting a different tonality in each conversation.

**The elements of your tonality you want to be conscious of are:**

Volume      Tempo            Rhythm

Inflection        Clarity

For example, someone that talks loud and fast may struggle developing rapport with someone who tends to speak slowly and quietly. You can use exactly the same words, but your tonality will dictate the way a message is received. Become aware of how you use your vocal qualities and then adjust them according to the situation.

## WORDS

Do you know what a word is? It is an internal marker used to describe an external concept. What does that mean? It means one of two things. Either we use the same words to describe different experiences, or we use different words to describe the same experiences. Occasionally we all match up, but to assume that may cause certain challenges.

Take the words often, regularly and sometimes for example. What do each of them mean to you? They all represent a frequency of occurrence, but how often is often? How regular is regular? How many times is sometimes? I enjoy running, and I regularly run once or twice per week. I have a friend who also runs regularly, every March 24th, regular as clockwork!

When you are using language, be aware that different words can mean different things to different people. If you are trying to build rapport, it is important to use the language and wording of your prospect. For example:

| Prospect: | *I need it urgently* |
|---|---|
| Salesperson 1: | *We'll send it quickly* |
| Salesperson 2: | *We'll send it urgently* |

Who is likely to have a better relationship with the prospect? You might argue that each response is the same, and in fact, both salespeople may be able to deliver at the same time, but salesperson 1 will have broken the communication pattern with his prospect. Why? Who knows, but that is not the question. Perhaps the prospect has recently had issues with delivery times and is looking for a priority delivery arrangement. Perhaps someone promised to get something delivered quickly but then it ended up being late. You don't need to know why, you just need to recognise the language that your prospect uses is a representation of their internal thought processes.

## HOW TO USE THE CONCEPTS OF RAPPORT

Matching and mirroring is not the only way you can use these ideas to build rapport. In fact, it is important to know that these techniques will actually cause you to lose rapport in about 15% of situations. In order to give you the best chance for rapport success, here are the 3 ways to use these concepts effectively.

## MATCHING AND MIRRORING

If your prospect is sat upright with their legs crossed, matching will have you doing the same to the very last detail. Mirroring will have you crossing your left leg when their right leg is crossed. Fairly straight forward so far? Good, then let me complicate it a little.

Many NLP trainers will teach you that you need to match exactly to gain rapport, and also as soon as someone changes position, you need to change position too. Now whilst this may be good for a clinical situation, try that in a sales meeting and you will quickly be looking for a new prospect. So how do you do it?

The answer is be comfortable and use natural breaks to change position. Try this for a moment. Cross your arms normally. Good. Now cross your arms over the other way. No, I said the other way. That was probably the same way again. (I appreciate that doing this when reading probably wasn't easy, maybe I should have said cross your legs instead... yes, try that too, cross you legs and then cross them the other way!).

Well, whichever limbs you decided to cross, no doubt the second way felt completely awkward. Would you ever want to feel that way in a sales meeting just because a NLP book told you to do so? No, then don't do it. If they cross their legs, you cross your legs as you feel comfortable, same with your arms, and any other postures your prospect decides to get into.

Also, you do not need to match and mirror every aspect. For example, if your prospect puts his feet up on the desk, it is not good rapport building skills to do the same. Same if they pick their nose or scratch themselves inappropriately. Be selective with what you match, and stick to the more general postures and gestures.

Timing is the other challenge. Trying to match and mirror at the exact time your prospect changes may work in clinical situations, but in sales it is the awkward equivalent of the yawn and stretch move you used when you were sixteen and on a date at the cinema. Prospects know that sales people will attempt to match and mirror body language, so you need to be a little more subtle.

Instead, use natural breaks in the flow of a conversation to adjust your position. If your prospect has shifted, ask a question, sit forward and take a drink, then when you sit back, adopt the new posture that is appropriate to continue rapport. Don't be in a rush to change positions, but don't leave it too long either.

What about group rapport? Well, it is not possible to match and mirror everyone in the group, so pick the people you need to get on your side the most, and take an aspect from each of them. Chances are your group of prospects will be in rapport with each other, so you may be able to match one aspect and capture them all. Otherwise, use one persons arm gestures, another's leg crossing and the other's posture. Just remember to keep it natural.

---

## CROSS MATCHING

If someone is really aware of your using body language to build rapport, it is possible to use cross matching. This is where you reflect an element of their physiology with a different body part. For example, they have your legs crossed but you have your eyes crossed (I meant arms. Cross your arms, not your eyes!).

Milton Erickson, one of the people that Bandler and Grinder modelled when creating NLP, once cross-matched someone's heart beat with the tapping of his finger. Once he had got into rapport (paced) he was then able to lead his subject into a state of relaxation by slowing the rate at which he tapped his finger. This is a great example of how cross matching can work, so be prepared to use it, especially if someone is watching your body language closely.

## MIS-MATCHING

In my experience, around about 15% of the population are mis-matchers. We will cover this characteristic more in the section on meta-programmes, but for now, just understand that some people don't want to get into rapport with you through body language. Its not that you cant get into rapport with them, its just that if you try and match their physiology, they will shift so that they are back in a different position to you.

I am sure you have probably met people like this. No matter how hard you try and get them into rapport with you, they just don't join in. So you try harder, then you get flustered and then you panic and then you lose the sale. It doesn't have to be this way. Just accept that some people don't want to match body language.

If you try to change your position a couple of times and find that your prospect instantly shifts or gets uncomfortable, chances are you have a mis-matcher. In these situations, don't worry about physiological matching and mirroring, just get on with your sales pitch as normal. They will get into rapport with you when they are ready to do so.

## POSITIVE MISMATCHING

At some point, once you have rapport with your prospect, you need to take control of the conversation and steer it in the direction you want to go. This is when mismatching can be used constructively. Consider the following examples:

- End a communication you feel has no further purpose;

- Gain attention;

- Redirect the flow of conversation;

- Positively interrupt a communication for whatever purpose.

Trying to do each of these whilst maintaining rapport would probably be quite challenging. However, by artfully mismatching, you can maintain rapport and continue the conversation as you see fit.

How? Well, if you alter your physiology, tonality or words, you will mismatch. To end communication, try speaking quicker and in a higher tone. To gain attention, try speaking loudly with a bold gesture. You will need to develop your own styles of mismatching, and you probably have a number that you already use, you may just not have realised you were already mismatching.

Mismatching intentionally when you start to lead the conversation will allow you to see if you have maintained rapport at a crucial time. For example, lets say you are now going to switch from asking questions about your prospect to telling them about your product or service. This is you taking the lead on the conversation, and so you need to have sufficient rapport for them to stay with you in the conversation.

At this time, you need to change something, and check your prospect's reaction. For example, let's say you sit forward and raise the tempo of the conversation. How does your prospect react? If they sit forward and get into the conversation too then the chances are you have a good level of rapport. If they remain sat back and relaxed, then maybe you don't have the level of rapport you thought.

Prospects are not generally interested in your offering unless they feel you understand them sufficiently to be able to really offer them something of value. If you don't keep rapport when you lead, then you probably have missed something that your prospect deems important. If so, its back to the questioning and rapport-building stage for you.

So, there you have the first stage of developing rapport with your prospect. Early in the sales meeting, find a way to pace your prospect, focusing on aspects of your physiology, tonality and phraseology that you can adjust, allowing you to match and mirror. You have to pace before you can lead, so ensure you work on the rapport before you begin to direct the conversation along the path you wish to take.

However, I want you to understand that the above techniques only deliver superficial levels of rapport. If you watch a group of friends spending time together, you will notice that they all match and mirror unconsciously. Some will be sat in the same positions, others will be gesturing in the same ways and they will all have similar tempo in the way they speak with each other. This matching and mirroring therefore happens as an effect of being in rapport, rather than causing it.

There is no denying that matching and mirroring plays a part in developing rapport. In fact, if you do not match and mirror, you have a very good chance of developing no rapport. However, you need to get to a point where, like the group of friends, that aspect happens unconsciously. We will explore the various depths of rapport later when we look at the logical levels model.

For now, remember that the way you look, move and sound communicates as much as 93% of your message. Get this right at the start of the sales meeting and you give yourself a great chance of success as it develops.

## SKILLS REQUIRED - SENSORY ACUITY & BEHAVIOURAL FLEXIBILITY

> *"The successful man will profit from his mistakes and try again in a different way."*

**- Dale Carnegie**

> *"I have learned that success is to be measured not so much by the position that one has reached in life as by the obstacles which he has had to overcome while trying to succeed."*

**- Booker T. Washington**

To be good at getting into rapport, you must have a keen sense on whether what you are doing is working. This means, you need to be in tune with your prospect, listening keenly and also taking notice of any and all non-verbal indicators that are being given off.

Believe it or not (and I know I am not talking about you here!), but some sales people do not do this. They are too busy worrying about what to say next, or thinking about which feature to demonstrate in a minute, or thinking about the drive to their next appointment. Whatever has them distracted, they miss key bits of information about whether or not they are building rapport.

Sensory acuity, as we mentioned in the pillars of NLP section, is the ability to notice subtle changes in people or the environment. Behavioural Flexibility is knowing what changes to make whatever direction the conversation is going.

For example, you start listing features of your product and your prospect goes from sitting forward to leaning back in his chair, checking his watch and looking out the window. If you have good sensory acuity (and this is an easy one for sure) then you will pick up on this change.

**Note** - it is important to say at this point that we have no idea why our prospect has made this shift. We are assuming that if their change of behaviour coincided with us changing our activity that the two are linked, but this is not always the case.

Behavioural flexibility in this situation could be any of the following:

- Stop listing features and instead talk about the benefits and impact to the prospect and their situation;

- Check in with the prospect to make sure that you are being respectful of their time and that they are not expecting another appointment;

- Ask the prospect directly why he or she has disengaged and push them for a response.

Some of these solutions will be more suitable in some situations than others so choose your own behavioural flexibility response. For example, how would you respond to the below situations:

- You start to go through your presentation and your prospect starts yawning;

- You are meeting with two people and one person answers all of the questions, even when you ask the other person directly;

- Your prospect informs you that instead of having the two hours you were promised, you only have 5 minutes for the meeting;

- You rely on an internet connection for your sales presentation and your internet or wifi connections fail;

- You are about to start your sales presentation after building up the anticipation and the fire alarm goes off.

It is vital that you develop both sensory acuity as well as behavioural flexibility.

The Law of Requisite Variety from Cybernetics states that the person with the most flexibility in any given context will control the situation.

Think of a chess player for example. A better chess player is one that knows what outcomes can arise in advance and there can play a greater variety of possible winning moves than his competitor.

Alternatively, take the idea (true or not) that Inuit-Yupik people have many different words for snow, whereas the English language just has 'snow'. This would explain why people of the Arctic are able to survive far more effectively in snowy environments. They are able to distinguish between snow that is good for walking on, for melting to make drinking water and for building with for example. If I went to the Arctic, I wouldn't last five minutes.

The more flexibility you have in any situation, the more control you will be able to exert. Think about all of the different questions you can ask to get your prospect to understand your unique selling points. What about all the different ways you can close a meeting? Maybe it is your ability to understand people's meta-programmes and be able to sell to them specifically with their kind of language? Whatever you do, commit to giving yourself more options in the areas you are currently struggling to control.

# SKILLS REQUIRED - EYE ACCESSING CUES

*"I'm reading your eyes. The eyes can't lie. Didn't you know?! A quick lesson in lying. See, this is what us real cops do. We study liars.*

*Example: If I ask you a question about something visual, like your favourite colour, your eyes go up and to the left. Neurophysiology tells us your eyes go in that direction because you're accessing the visual cortex. So you're telling the truth. If your eyes go up and right, you're accessing the brain's creative centers and we know you're full of shit."*

**- Samuel L Jackson -** *The Negotiator*

Can you tell if someone is lying just by where their eyes look?

I remember one of the first times I taught the concept of eye accessing cues. It was the night after a new television show had started which was about the CIA and their techniques of interrogating suspects. During this initial episode (which it would appear my whole class had watched), the CIA operative asked a series of questions to the suspect before finally asking the one question he had been leading up to all along, "what are you doing in the United States?" Before the suspect had chance to even open his mouth, the CIA operative knew he was a liar!

How is this possible? Well, there is evidence to show that the way you move your eyes when asked to recall an experience will indicate how you are accessing that information. In fact, it can be very difficult to remember certain information without moving your eyes. Try answering these questions and be aware of your eye movements.

- What colour was your first bicycle?

- What sound does your front door make?

- What does it feel like to be alone?

The chances are your eyes moved as you accessed those memories in your mind. Now try answering these questions and see if you notice a difference.

---

- What would you look like dressed in a chicken suit riding a unicycle?

- What would your mobile phone sound like underwater?

- What would it feel like to be massaged by your favourite Hollywood superstar?

Was there a difference this time around?

If you have read the questions carefully, you will notice two aspects. Each of the questions relates to one of your primary senses; visual, auditory or kinaesthetic. You will probably have noticed that for each of these questions, your eyes moved in different directions. The other difference is that the first set of three questions asked you for a memory, but the second set of questions asked you to imagine something new.

The eye accessing cues are an indication to the sense that it being accessed and whether the response is being remembered or created. Each of the senses has a particular area, and you will look to one side to remember and the other to create thoughts. Let's have a look at these areas and explore what they mean.

**Note** - Always Calibrate! These cues are for a typical right handed person. Left handed people often store time differently and you may find that they invert from left to right for recall and construct. Always calibrate before making assumptions by asking a calibration such as the ones asked to you previously. A calibration question is one which controls the sense and whether it was recalled or constructed so that during the response you can observe the eye movements of your prospect.

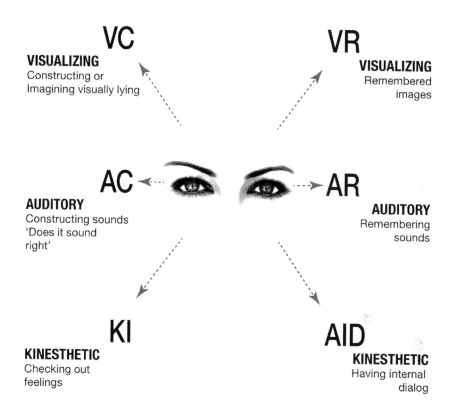

# CONSTRUCTED

# REMEMBERED

## VC
**VISUALIZING**
Constructing or
Imagining visually lying

## VR
**VISUALIZING**
Remembered
images

## AC
**AUDITORY**
Constructing sounds
'Does it sound
right'

## AR
**AUDITORY**
Remembering
sounds

## KI
**KINESTHETIC**
Checking out
feelings

## AID
**KINESTHETIC**
Having internal
dialog

**VISUAL RECALL**

This is where you remember an image from the past, something that actually happened to you. Remember the question about your first bicycle? If you have normal eye accessing cues, you would have looked up and to you left. Typically, the harder it is to remember, the more exaggerated the eye movement. A simple question will require minimal eye movement, whereas a really tough question could leave people staring in that direction for seconds or minutes.

## VISUAL CONSTRUCT

This is the area that allows you to create images in your mind. This does not always mean that you are lying however. For example, if someone held up a jumper and asked you if it would suit them, you may want to imagine them wearing that jumper before responding. In that case, you would have to create an image of this person wearing the jumper so that you could make up your mind. You may also find that people with strong auditory or kinaesthetic preferences have to create more images if they are asked visual-based questions.

## AUDITORY RECALL

To remember a sound, you normally look towards your left ear. This horizontal eye-accessing cue should be easy to remember as the eyes move towards the very organs responsible for the auditory sense. You may even notice the head follows the eyes for auditory questions as these can be difficult for people to remember that do not have a strong auditory preference.

## AUDITORY CONSTRUCT

Creating sounds in your imagination will require you to look towards your right ear. You may access this area if you are reading sheet music for the first time or have just ordered some concert tickets and are wondering what the atmosphere is going to be like.

## KINAESTHETIC

When you look down and to the right, this is the place you will access your emotions and feelings. Your imagination tends to slow down in this position, allowing you focus on what you feel and what that means to you. These emotions are also likely to be accompanied by the appropriate facial expressions.

## AUDITORY INTERNAL DIALOGUE

This is where you look when you want to have a conversation with yourself. When that little voice inside your head kicks in, this is the easiest place to listen to it. Don't believe me? Try looking down left now and listen to what it is up to... it rarely rests or shuts up!

## HOW CAN YOU USE THIS IN A SALES CONTEXT?

Rarely are you going to use this understanding of eye accessing cues in a sales meeting to check if your prospect is lying to you. However, if you can identify the modalities that are being accessed for key questions, you can get good insights into the context of the conversation.

- If you ask a question about a project, and someone looks directly left, then the chances are that person is remembering something that was told to them. If so, who was the other person in that conversation? Are they important in the decision making process.

- If you ask a technical question and someone looks up and left, perhaps they are remembering a schematic diagram. If so, why not ask if you can see the same diagram rather than asking them to describe it.

- If you ask a question and your prospect looks down right, then there is probably some emotion attached to either the situation or the outcome. Follow up by asking them what it would mean to get this right first time.

- If you ask a question and someone looks down left, perhaps they are thinking things through in their head. Don't interrupt, but when they look back at you, perhaps you can ask them to explain their thought process.

Use the eye accessing cues to help you ask questions to the right representation system. If you ask visual questions to someone who processes primarily in their auditory sense, you will soon break rapport. Remember, its not about your preference, its about theirs!

# NEUROLOGICAL LEVELS RAPPORT

**IDENTITY**
*Who?*

How do you see yourself in a particular situation?
Identity may be easier to express as a metaphor.
How would you describe yourself in a given role?

**VALUES**
*Why?*

Values drive all decisions and hence behaviour.
Understanding someone's values will give you an
understanding of their motivation.

**BELIEFS**
*Why?*

Our beliefs determine the actions we take in
order to realise our values. Beliefs are typically
generalisations of if/then statements.

**CAPABILITIES**
*How?*

Your skill set and knowledge will influence
your behaviour. Developing your skills will
give you a wider range of behaviour choices.

**BEHAVIOR**
*What?*

How do you spend your time? What are the
main activities with which you fill your time?
What are you saying and doing?

**ENVIRONMENT**
*Where?*

Environment is everything outside of you,
from the clothes you wear to your physical
location and also the situation or context.

This model is adapted from the original model created by Robert Dilts. The model proposes that the level of neurology involved is greater at the top (identity) than at the bottom (environment). Keep in mind that making a change in your behaviour or environment will not necessarily impact your identity. However, change your identity or values, and you will see massive shifts in the behaviour and results that ensue. Can you see now why so many training courses don't create the desired results?

When you go for a drink with your friends, do you focus on matching and mirroring your body language? Do you study their every movement to make sure you are sitting in the same position, reaching for your drink at the same time and attempting to breathe in time in case your friendship deteriorates and the person sat beside you mistakes you for a stranger?

I hope you can see how ridiculous this situation would be, and yet even without thinking about your physiology and tonality, there exists a level of rapport that continues in spite of whatever else is going on. In fact, if you watch a group of friends, you will see that they do match and mirror their body language and the way they talk with each other. However, this is happening at an unconscious level rather than being something they are aware of. If body language was the only way to be in rapport, what could explain this connection?

The fact is that rapport is a state that occurs naturally between people who have a proper relationship. When you have a real connection with someone, the matching of body movement, tonality and linguistics happens at an unconscious level because the connection exists at a much higher level of awareness.

Sure, we can use matching to help us create a superficial level of rapport, but if you want to develop a proper relationship and connection, you will need to understand what these higher levels of awareness and are how to access them when developing rapport.

Once you have established this advanced rapport, you have a greater amount of flexibility within the relationship. For example, if you have a significant disagreement with a prospect on your first meeting, the chances of turning that situation around for the better is going to be a challenge. However, you can have a shouting match with someone close to you and yet a day later everything is back to normal.

So how are these levels of awareness structured? These are the Neurological Levels that were originally developed by Robert Dilts. In the

---

neurological levels model, Dilts describes the levels of ever-deepening psychological concepts that occur in both conscious and unconscious awareness.

If we want to develop rapport at a deeper level, we need to understand how to put this model into action.

## ENVIRONMENT

Environment can be described as everything from the skin out. One of the easiest things for a sales person to control in their environment is their appearance and how they dress. Are you dressing appropriately for your sales meetings? And by 'appropriately', I don't necessarily mean in a suit and tie.

For example, there is a huge difference between the digital marketing world and the realm of financial services. I remember one of my finance clients being very particular about the type of shirts that had to be worn by the sales people; cotton double cuff shirts with no breast pocket. In the digital marketing world however, for example, you could be overdressed in a nice cardigan and smart T-shirt.

What makes your dress sense 'acceptable' is really not down to your role or the company that you work for. Rather it is about the expectations of the person you are meeting, your prospect – how do they want to be made to feel?

Let's say you are selling financial services products. What's that first impression that you want to give your potential client? If you are selling mortgages, insurance and pensions, you probably want them to think you are professional, that you are going to take care of their money and that you are an upstanding citizen in good standing. If you turn up in jeans, trainers and a sweaty T-shirt, you are probably not going to convey that impression. You turn up in a nice suit, in a nice shirt and tie, you are probably going to get a lot closer.

If you are meeting with a small business owner to discuss their accounting requirements and you turned up fully suited and booted, is that going to give them the right impression? Sitting at somebody's kitchen dressed that way talking about their book keeping could cause them to feel that you are may be a little bit superior to them?

So, the case of clothing or the case of appearance comes down to what the expectations of the person you are going to meet and how do you want to make them feel. If you want them to feel that you are somebody who is in control and is formal and is always very precise, then maybe wearing a suit is important. If you want to have slightly softer or relaxed attitude, you want to approach people and you want them to feel comfortable discussing things with you, then maybe you dress that down slightly.

If you are unsure about your current appearance, I can highly recommend visiting an image consultant or a style consultant. I remember seeing one many years ago (some might say I due a repeat visit!) and she worked absolute wonders. We looked at the way I was currently dressing and the message I wanted to convey and created a plan. Once this set of rules was in place, I knew what to wear, the specific cuts and fits that I needed to buy, the colours and even down to the accessories that finished off the look. A very beneficial process.

## FIRST IMPRESSIONS COUNT!

Where do you hold your meetings? There is a well known story about James Caan one of the dragons from the BBC show Dragon's Den who, when he first started in business, wanted to have the appearance of success. He set up a recruitment company and rented a very, very small office in Pall Mall in the centre of London. Clients would come to meet with him at his office, see the location and be suitably impressed. However, because the office was so small, instead of ruining the illusion, instead he would say "we are a little bit busy in the office today, let me take you out for a coffee instead." In doing so, the clients would meet him at this posh address and have the right first impression but they never actually get to see his office and he could conduct his business off site. The environment gave the initial impression of massive success even though, behind the scenes, that was not necessarily the case.

So, where you hold your meetings and how you dress up is vitally important in creating that first impression, the first feeling that your potential buyer is going to get from you. If you are able to then you need to be in control of your environment. It may seem picky, but even down to the temperature of your meeting room and how people feel in that environment. Keep it nice and warm, provide them with water, and provide comfortable chairs. Think about Maslow's hierarchy of needs. If basic physiological needs are not catered for, your sales pitch will not be first thing on your prospect's mind.

## BEHAVIOUR

The behaviour level of the neurological levels model is where you find matching and mirroring of body language and physiology that we have already covered. We can match elements of Physiology, Tonality or Words to help develop rapport with our prospects. Remember, a common misconception is that you have to match and mirror at exactly the same time as your prospect is moving. Whilst there is some strong evidence to support the matching and mirroring concept, I am also going to suggest to you that when you see a group of friends, the body language matching may actually be a result of the rapport rather than the cause.

Let's imagine for a moment that we go to a social engagement. We head out to a bar with a group of friends and as we all sit around the table, there is an element of synchronicity. When I reach for drink, a friend of mine reaches for drink; when I put it back, they put it back; I sit forwards, a few minutes later all of us will sit forward. There is always one guy who sat back and is always in a different position (mis-matcher). We will come back to him later when we discuss meta-programs, but things tend to synchronise if you are in a group of friends. Now, you are not matching and mirroring to create rapport. Instead, these movements are a by-product or symptom of the rapport you and your friends already have at a higher level. We will explore these throughout the rest of the neurological levels concepts.

This is where normal rapport lessons finish. However, something tells me you want to learn the juicy stuff of how to develop unbreakable rapport with people you have never even met! If so, read on.

## CAPABILITIES AND SKILLS

If you have a unique talent and you meet someone else with the same skill, there will be an element of rapport. Let's take, for example, unicyclists.

I was in Bath, England one Christmas period and as I walked amidst the throngs of festive shoppers, three unicyclists went past me on the street. Now normally when you have groups of people engaging in the same activity, there is some element that is similar about them from an outside perspective. You may expect them to look similar, dress in the same sort of clothes or be of similar ages.

However, here were three people, all of whom had the skill of being able to unicycle, but all of them were completely different individuals. There was an older guy, there was a middle-aged guy, and then there was a younger guy too. They were all dressed completely differently.

The one element they definitely shared was that they all enjoyed to and had the ability to unicycle. People with skills in common tend to hang out together, either when learning the particular skill or once they have mastered it. If you go to a training course, often times there is a lot of rapport that's built instantly whether or not an icebreaker is done at the beginning with the group.

Therefore, people with similar skills and capabilities will tend to be able to develop rapport even if there is mismatching at more superficial levels.

## BELIEFS

Your unique view of the world may allow you to create connections and develop rapport with the people you meet. For beliefs level rapport, the classic example is going to a church or any other religious environment.

If you have been to a church recently, there are stages of a church. Walking in at the back, you first have those kids who go to church but necessarily don't want to be there. Potentially their parents have dragged them there and they are only going to hang out at the back trying not to cause too much trouble. They are still kind of engaging to some extent and they will sing their hymns under their breaths, they don't want to appear uncool.

If you move forward slightly, you will find a young couple. Maybe they have been dating for a while or maybe they are newlyweds. They have been involved in the church for some time and they still want to show up, but maybe they can't show up every weekend. Move forward some more and you see the big family, the parents and the children they are all dressed in their Sunday best because this is their day of the week where they get to bond and they get to come together under their belief of religion.

And at the very front of the congregation you have the old people. For them, it is either their time to really start believing in religion and it's almost like a negotiation session – "Do I get this? Do I get that? Okay, great, this is the religion for me." Alternatively, they have been going to church their whole life and have graduated from the back of the church all the way to that front pew.

If you get to the front of the room and you turn around what you see is a whole raft of different people that look very different; different skin tones, different creeds, different languages being spoken. They are all sat slightly differently – some have sat forward, some have sat back. They are dressed in an assortment of outfits and their appearances are all very different.

What brings all of these people together is their belief - their beliefs about religion and spirituality. So, at any point they can have a conversation and there would be no need to match and mirror body language. It would just be a natural conversation because they have this thing in common.

So, if you have beliefs that are similar to that of your prospect, you should try to uncover them. I can remember being in a sales situation once in a very small car service garage in Birmingham. The meeting was not going well. We had been made to wait for ages and the meeting kept getting interrupted and it got to a point where the husband had to leave the meeting. We couldn't really continue at that point so we made some small talk and were looking the small reception area and on the desk of this office was a flyer for a local church. The sales person I was with picked it up and said "My mom goes to that church" and I have never seen a U-turn in a meeting happen quite like this. The eyes of the woman lit up and for the next 20 minutes, all she could talk about was her church, her church, her church. Her husband came in after about 10 minutes and they actually stood together with their arms around them, each other talking about their passions and their beliefs of the church and invited both of us. I didn't live in the area, so I couldn't attend but this girl said that she had been to the church many a times and that her mom was still a regular. After that we got back into the sales conversation, the meeting went very differently with the sale being made at the end of it. There was a different level of rapport. In that short exchange we moved from the relationship from sales person and prospect to a connection of people who have similar beliefs resulting in a far deeper level of rapport.

## VALUES

The way to figure out somebody's values is to ask them what is important to them. "What is important to you about life?" For example, would give you someone's core values that drive their life. Another way to do it is to look at the activities that somebody engages on a regular basis. How people spend their time, money and resources will give you a very good reflection of what is important to them in the given context and if you can get into a values level rapport with a prospect, this is probably the deepest level of rapport that you can get on to with somebody as a sales person.

For example, let's say we visit someone's office and we can see that they engage in sailing on a regular occasion. I remember sitting in a sales meeting at the start of my sales career where the MD had pictures of his boat all over his office. It didn't take a genius to realise he was a keen sailor. However, what I didn't know was the values that sailing fulfilled for him.

*"What is it about sailing that you like?"*

*"What do you get out of sailing?"*

Both of these questions will give you access to his values. You may get a response about how they love being away from everything, they love just the sounds of nature, they love the occasional silence followed by crushing of waves and they just love being outdoors and it's just being them and the elements.

Old school sales rapport would teach you to find something in common with your prospect and then expand upon it. I have seen experienced sales people trying to build rapport by asking questions about "what do you do?" and after 10 minutes of futile questioning find nothing in common. In the end, they will simply take anything and latch onto it and they will pretend that

that's something that they do in an attempt to create rapport. "You play the violin? I love playing the violin!" for example.

If you understand the values behind why people do what they do, I guarantee that it doesn't matter what the activity or behaviour, you will be able to create a deep level of rapport.

So, even though I don't sail (although it is something on my list of things to do), I know that I can use a values level conversation to develop rapport with this prospect based on the fact that I know he likes being outdoors in nature and that it is important to him to be able to get away from everything. You may even find that by talking about how you have similar values, you start bouncing ideas about of other ways to meet this value at even greater levels. (Just be sure you can maintain this rapport when you start moving into the more sales related aspect of your meeting!)

This technique is called a values alignment and it allows you to develop a deep rapport by mapping your values over onto someone else's behaviours. Simply identify your prospect's values and then tell a related story from your own experience.

So, if this person likes being away in nature and likes just getting out in that boat and just likes being disconnected from it all, I might talk about a camping trip or when I went bear-hunting in Yellowstone Park (I had my camera and no bears were hurt in the making of this book). I might talk about that time when I went somewhere so far away and it was so quiet, all I could hear was the sound of my breathing and even the trees didn't make a noise.

How many times do we actually get into this level of rapport with someone, to a point where we know what drives them to take action? Instead, we keep the conversation superficial and at a level where you are not likely to offend anyone. However, you need to develop emotion during a sale, and values are the ultimate emotions people are looking to experience.

Develop a values-level rapport with someone and the superficial aspects of appearance and body language fade into insignificance.

## IDENTITY

Identity level rapport is the highest level of rapport that you can possibly get into. This is where you see yourself as being part of the same object or part of the same metaphor. A classic example is in the 2006 European Football Championships, Christiano Ronaldo and Wayne Rooney where engaged in the 'Winkgate' scandal where Ronaldo winked at Rooney as he was sent off. At that time they were both playing for Manchester United, and there was the question of whether they would ever be able to play again together on the same team after what had happened. Surely there was no way they would be able get into the same level of rapport which you need to have on a team as they would have done before this scandal.

After the tournament and back at Manchester United, training behind closed doors must have been pretty tense, but then the first game of the season took place. The Manchester United team looked incredible, but it was the chemistry between Rooney and Ronaldo that was phenomenal. They instinctively knew where each other was going to be on the pitch. They were just in complete and total rapport despite the scandal.

This was due to their identity. The second they donned the Manchester United shirts, everything else ceased to be important. The only thing that mattered to them was being part of the Manchester United team. There were no differences of opinion, and the 'Winkgate' scandal was pushed aside. It simply didn't matter. What was important was representing their team and getting the result.

Can you imagine this sort of thing happening in a sales meeting and you being able to maintain rapport with a prospect? It would be very difficult unless you too were part of the same team.

As you move higher through the neurological levels, you develop a deeper level of rapport. It then doesn't matter about everything else that comes below. If you can get into values level rapport or identity level rapport, do you think it matters what clothes you are wearing, whether you cross your legs or your arms or whether you break eye contact? Of course it doesn't. The deeper the level of rapport, the greater flexibility you have to mismatch at the more superficial levels.

## IS IT POSSIBLE TO GET INTO RAPPORT IMMEDIATELY?

You know those times when you meet people and it seems as if you have known them forever. Is there a way to develop that level of rapport instantly with strangers that would assist in building the relationship right from the start?

I would say that there are three main ways of generating immediate rapport with people, although the last one is a little risky for salespeople to try.

## ASSUME RAPPORT

This approach suggests that rather than trying to develop rapport, just act as if you already have it. Although this may sound simple, you will be surprised how many sales people think that you have to develop rapport before you can start talking about your product.

## DO YOUR RESEARCH

Find out what you can about your prospect before the meeting. Connect with them on social media, read their blog if they have one and discover as much information about this person as you can ahead of your sales meeting. This way, not only do you appear to have put in the effort, you also have plenty of ways to develop the rapport.

## NOT DEVELOP RAPPORT

I know this sounds crazy, but what if you made the prospect get into rapport with you? Remember we described rapport in NLP as pacing and then leading. Well what would happen if you just did the leading part and forced them to get into rapport with you? As I mentioned, this technique is a little risky for sales people, unless you are in the very top of your class or if you tend to sell to groups where trying to match and mirror everyone would be impossible.

In these ways, you can develop a superficial level of rapport immediately. However, make sure you continue to develop the relationship throughout your meeting.

## UNDERSTANDING WHO IS IN FRONT OF YOU

One of the most important lessons I learned when studying NLP was that, even though we all speak the same language, individuals have different communication preferences. As soon as I realised all of the different ways of using the same words, it shined a huge light on so many of the problems I had had in relationships in the past.

As you go through this section, I challenge you to think back to some of the problems you may have previously faced and see whether, if you had known these different preferences at the time, you might have been able to communicate in a way that would have been more effective.

When selling, understanding the communication preferences of your prospect is essential in both maintaining rapport and also being able to present your solution effectively towards the end of a sales meeting. If you get it wrong and communicate outside of your prospect's preferences, you will be unnecessarily testing your rapport as your client struggles to understand the information you are putting across. If you put across the wrong information at the end of the meeting and miss the mark with your final presentation, you will be making your job of closing more difficult than it needs to be.

Each one of us experiences the world in a different way and this is dependent on our sensory filters. Two people can experience the exact same event, but because of their programming and conditioning, will react in completely different ways. You and I might simply walk past a bin on the street, but to someone from the musical Stomp they might see a musical instrument and a vehicle for creativity. Some people might hear about a slump in the economic market and get depressed at the thought of their dwindling pension value, whereas others will see that exact same event as the opportunity to make a killing in the markets.

There really are so many different preferences dependent on the context and situations that arise, and if you understand your preferences and that of your prospect, you can communicate more effectively. One of the simplest examples is the argument of the glass half-full vs half empty. At the extremes, it does not matter how much one person tries to influence the other, they will never understand (or at least admit to) the perspective of the other person. To the outsider, with an objective view, they are both correct. However, if you are sitting on one side of the fence, it is a struggle to connect with someone on the other side.

You may be thinking this is trivial but have you ever been in a situation with someone who is overly positive or negative in such a way that it becomes irritating? What is it like to communicate with such a person? Do they seem obnoxious? Only interested in their own opinion and what they have to say? Don't understand your point of view?

Now imagine the opportunity to get this wrong with over 50 different types of preference. With more than 50 different ways you can show lack of understanding and poor communication skills, there is a clear need to develop our understanding of the different people patterns so that we can avoid these situations. All you need is some awareness and a small amount of behavioural flexibility and you will be able to become significantly more effective in your ability to communicate with anyone.

Your goal should be to become a communication chameleon, able to change your language subtly in order to be able to connect with any person who sits in front of you. This will enable you to sell to far more people than you currently do. And the good news is, you only need to know a few patterns to make a significant improvement.

## META PROGRAMS

Every second, our senses are being bombarded with millions of tiny bits of information, most of which we are not even aware of. Think about it, if you tried to concentrate on everything around you at this very moment, you would literally go crazy.

Some of the pieces of information your senses are picking up are obvious. As you are reading this then I am guessing your visual sense is working well and you are able to read the words, but if you allow your focus to soften slightly, then you will see all of the other things going on around this page of the book that previously you may have been unaware of. You may be conscious of the weight of this book as you read it, but were you aware of the feeling of your clothes against your legs and arms as you do so? (Presupposition you are wearing clothes!)

In order to make sense of the world and not go crazy, your conscious mind has created three coping strategies. Whilst the unconscious mind takes in all of the information, the conscious mind has a limit to what it can retain, which as you will discover later, will also impact our ability to recall information. The coping strategies are:

*Delete*      *Distort*      *Generalise*

## DELETE

One of the simplest ways to reduce the amount of information entering our brain is simply to delete some of it. In fact, your brain has a Reticular Activating System (or RAS) that allows you to program which bits to delete and which bits to let in.

As we have already discussed, there are some bits of information that are not necessary to our every day life. If you didn't focus on the feeling of your clothes against your skin then you would probably still get through life with no major problems. However, if you were wearing a brand new cashmere jumper then you may be drawn to the feeling a little more often.

The classic example happens with cars, and if you have ever bought a new car for yourself, you will be able to attest to this. You visit the showroom and see a gorgeous car, one that you know will draw the attention of everyone and make you look incredible. You get in, take it for a little test drive and decide to buy it there and then on the spot (you impulse buyer you!). You drive it away, waving at the salesman as he or she quickly becomes a speck in your rear view mirror, and you take the car immediately to a road where you can find out what it really does (we have all done that, right?).

What happens next can only be described as magic. It somehow appears that as you were buying your new car, suddenly, hundreds of other people went out and bought exactly the same car as you! How is that possible?

This is the reticular activating system kicking in. It is not that suddenly everybody bought your car. Instead, those cars were always there, but now because you have programmed your brain to say your model of car is more important, your brain will now pay more attention to those kinds of cars.

When you decide that something is more important or has a higher value in your life, your reticular activating system will prioritise this information into your awareness. This means that you will start seeing more of these things everywhere you go.

If you are in field sales, a great technique is to train yourself to look for new leads as you are driving around. The more you practise this, the more leads you will begin to notice. If you keep a camera or a dictaphone on you at all times, you will be able to take a note of these potential prospects as you are in between appointments.

Another concept that suggests we delete surplus information is Miller's Law, after George A. Miller. His research suggested that the short-term memory is only capable of holding seven plus or minus two ($7 \pm 2$) chunks of information. A chunk is the largest meaningful unit in the presented material that the person recognises.

For example, remembering each digit in an eleven-digit phone number may be challenging, but if you group the numbers into pairs or threes, it suddenly becomes a lot easier. When someone reads this phone number back to you in different chunks, it is possible that you will not even recognise your own number.

## DISTORT

When we distort information, we are looking to make it fit with our existing map of the world. Rather than creating entirely new belief systems for every situation we find ourselves in, we tend to use our existing beliefs and occasionally push square pegs through round holes.

For example, have you ever found yourself staring at someone convinced that you know them? You may even shout out their name trying to draw their attention, only to find that when this person turns around, it is not the person you thought it was. (Cue awkward look of embarrassment and you pretending you were speaking to someone else that was stood next to them...)

Sometimes we make assumptions on a situation before we have all the facts, but this allows us to make faster decisions and interpretations. For example, let's say in the corner of the room right now is something that looks like a rope, but it could also be a snake. How do you behave? If you assume it is a rope, you will probably wander over and pick it up, no problems. However, if you think it is a snake, your behaviour is likely to be very different.

Your experience, situation and context will all play a part on the distortions you make. Taking the example above. British people are rarely exposed to snakes and poisonous creatures. If you take someone from England and put them in front of a garden hose, how would they react? Would they react differently if they were in their house versus in a rain forest? Would their behaviour differ if they had never seen a snake versus they had recently been bitten by a snake whilst on holiday.

It is important to keep in mind that context and experience will impact the distortions your prospect will be likely to make. If you need to control or impact these aspects, then make sure you do so.

## GENERALISE

Have you ever made a generalisation or used a stereotype? All French people love red wine or all Australians love a good barbecue. These are examples of your brain trying to limit the number of distinctions it needs to make about a given situation.

If we have enough experiences to reinforce a global conclusion, we will then generalise this new belief and apply it like a blanket to every subsequent example. Any time you use the word 'always' or 'never', you are making a generalisation.

For example, you and your significant other just move in together, and during that first week, you make the bed every morning. Towards the end of the week, you ask your partner "why don't you EVER make the bed?" Now, keep in mind that you have been together only a week, you have now made a generalisation that this person never makes the bed... ever! You then imagine the mess that was their bed before they were lucky enough to meet you. You even start looking from more examples of times when they do not make the bed.

This is generalisation gone wrong. However, it is scary to see how quickly we can create generalisations. It is even possible to make a global conclusion based on one experience if there is enough emotional intensity that surrounds the particular event.

Generalisations are useful however. If you have ever been to a fashion boutique and seen a designer chair that looks nothing like a chair, you were probably able to still sit down. You see it next to a table with a bottom-sized flat section, a possible back support and enough support to stop it falling to the ground and you figure it must be a chair.

Generalisations allow us to make assumptions about a situation that mean we can process information more quickly. However, you know what they say about assumptions!

## HOW WE DELETE & DISTORT

Meta programs are the internal filters that determine which information we will process and which we will delete and distort. Our brain has a preference in any given context as to which bits of information it thinks is necessary versus superfluous.

For example, three people can have the same experience of going to a music concert but their recollections of the experience will likely be completely different based on the information they decide to process. One might tell you all about the amazing stage set and the lighting effects and the fire that came out of the front of the stage. The second might tell you all about the lyrics, how if you listen to the words you can really understand how the writer was feeling at the time. The third may tell you all about the amazing people they met in the queue, when getting a drink and at the souvenir stand.

## SAME EXPERIENCE - THREE DIFFERENT STORIES.

The reason why lies in understanding meta programs. There are well over 50 meta programs in total, with more being identified constantly. You may even come up with some of your own as you read this section, or at least your own labels for them. We will explore 5 of the common meta programs in this book, and they are:

- Visual - Auditory - Kinaesthetic
- Towards - Away
- Internal - External
- Big Picture - Small Details
- Options - Procedures

## THE META PROGRAM SCALE

When you think about meta programs, avoid thinking of them as boxes. Instead, picture a sliding scale or continuum that runs between the extremes of each classification. Although you will likely have a preference towards one side in any given context, you are never exclusively that aspect.

## VISUAL - AUDITORY - KINAESTHETIC

*"I hear and I forget. I see and I remember. I do and I understand."*
**- Confucius**

One of the first concepts of NLP that people learn is that we all have a preference towards either our visual, auditory or kinaesthetic sense.

Think about the best way you learn for a moment. Do you find it easy to read something in a book and pick up the concepts or perhaps you can watch someone else do something and easily copy their actions? Perhaps you learn best in lectures or by listening to audio books and seminars? Maybe you need to get your hands dirty and actually give something a go before you really get it?

We all have preferences towards one of these senses, and we call our preferred sense our primary representation system. This is the sense through which we best process and retain information, but remember we all have the ability to use all of our senses.

Imagine for a moment if we only ever used our primary representation system; how would we be able to function? Visual people would never answer their mobile phones as they would not recognise their own ring tone. Auditory people would have to try every doorbell on the street before finding their own house. Kinaesthetic people would have to try on every jacket until they remember which one they were wearing.

So what are the characteristics of each of the representation systems?

## VISUAL PREFERENCE

- Thrive on visually presented information.
- Quick thinker and may speak rapidly - a picture paints a thousand words (all at the same time!).
- Hand movements at eye level or above.
- Sharp dressers with a good sense of colour.
- Observant of environmental detail with a neat and tidy workplace.
- May forget verbal instructions unless they're written down.

## AUDITORY PREFERENCE

- Like to talk things through.
- Likely to have good language skills.
- Use of specific words and voice tone is important.
- Can be easily distracted by noise.
- Speech is slow and considered and may speak rhythmically.
- Often have an internal dialogue with self.

## KINAESTHETIC PREFERENCE

- Touch people to get their attention.
- Strong awareness of physical proximity.
- Physically oriented and move and gesture a lot.
- Slow talkers, use gestures and expressions.
- May have messy handwriting.
- When inactive, tend to fidget.

With this in mind, sales presentations should aim to cover each element, with a stronger emphasis on your prospect's primary representation system.

In order to find out what your preferred representation system is, take the quick test below. Answer the questions quickly as your instinctive response is usually the most accurate. For each question, highlight the response which is closest to how you generally behave:

# VAK PREFERENCES TEST

**When learning a new skill, you prefer to:**
- (a) watch what the teacher is doing
- (b) listen to a detailed explanation from the teacher
- (c) take part in a practical exercise

**Your favourite activities include:**
- (a) films, photography, going to museums and exhibitions
- (b) listening to music, taking to friends, quiet time
- (c) taking part in sport, eating good food, dancing

**You remember things best by:**
- (a) keeping a written note or printed details
- (b) repeating things aloud or in my head over and over
- (c) doing or practising the activity

**You are most likely to say:**
- (a) I see what you mean
- (b) I hear what you are saying
- (c) I know how you feel

**You tend to speak:**
- (a) quick and excited
- (b) at a medium, rhythmic pace
- (c) slow and considered

**When you want to relax, you prefer to:**
- (a) watch television or read a magazine
- (b) listen to some music or the radio
- (c) take a long, steamy bath

**You tend to say:**
- (a) show me
- (b) tell me
- (c) let me try

**You first notice people:**
- (a) appearance and dress
- (b) vocal qualities and tonality
- (c) posture and how they hold themselves

**You can tell someone is lying because:**
- (a) you notice they look a particular way
- (b) you hear a change in their voice or tone
- (c) you get a feeling in your gut

**You buy a new coat because:**
- (a) you look good it in
- (b) the assistant tells you it suits you
- (c) it feels warm and comfortable

## NOW ADD UP HOW MANY A'S, B'S AND C'S YOU SELECTED.

**Mostly A's?** You have a VISUAL preference. You prefer diagrams and handouts that allow you to see the information being presented to you. Mind maps and flow charts help you picture how concepts fit together. You probably pick up information quite quickly, and communicate it to others even faster. You are conscious of your image and like to make a good first impression.

**Mostly B's?** You have a AUDITORY preference. For you, lectures and spoken explanations are your preferred communication styles. You probably enjoy silence and find background noise quite distracting. You speak with purpose, choosing your words carefully from your extensive vocabulary and delivering them with precision.

**Mostly C's?** You have a KINAESTHETIC preference. You like to be hands on and get stuck in. You are careful with your communication, considering how you feel about what you are going to say and the likely impact it will have on the feelings of others. You make decisions based on instinct, listening to your 'gut' on how best to proceed.

**No preference?** This means that you are able to utilise each of the senses to effectively process information. You may find that you have a preference for one over the others in given contexts - for example, you may prefer visual art but like to learn with audio products - but in general, you do not mind how information is presented to you.

## REPRESENTATION SYSTEMS IN SALES

So how can you tell a person's primary representation system without using such a test? The answer is in their language.

Linguistic predicates are verbs, adverbs, and adjectives that derive from certain sensory systems and will give you a good idea as to the primary representation system of your prospect. These words and phrases are used naturally in a person's vocabulary and are your key to know how to modify your sales pitch. Below is a list of common linguistic predicates for each representation system.

| Neutral | Visual | Auditory | Kinaesthetic |
|---------|--------|----------|--------------|
| manage | oversee | conduct | handle |
| understand | see | explain | run through |
| describe | outline | narrate | set out |
| identify | pinpoint | call attention to | put finger on |
| increase | enhance | amplify | intensify |
| ignore | overlook | tune out | pass over |
| eradicate | extinguish | silence | stamp out |
| appealing | picturesque | tuneful | fragile |
| tangible | visible | audible | concrete |
| attentive | focused | attuned | glued |
| surprised | dazzled | dumbfounded | shocked |
| confusing | fuzzy | garbled | jumbled |

If you notice your prospect is using a majority of one set of words, there is a good chance that it will tell you their preferred representation system. Combine that with what you now know about the other tendencies of Visual, Auditory and Kinaesthetic, and you should be able to tailor your sales pitch to best match their preferences.

So, what are some of the ways you can tailor your sales approach to appeal to the various representation systems?

## VISUAL PREFERENCE

- Your overall visual impression needs to be very good even before you begin your dialogue.
- Prepare plenty of visual descriptions of your product or solution.
- Visuals need to actually see the product or result of your service, so perhaps use videos of your product in your presentation.
- Get them to visualise themselves using your product or service.
- Make sure you have good eye contact with them.

## AUDITORY PREFERENCE

- Your tone of voice and other auditory qualities in the environment will have a big influence on them.
- They are particularly sensitive to extreme volumes and will pick up on any incongruity in your voice.
- Minimise the amount of distracting noise in the environment otherwise your prospect will not be paying you 100% attention.
- Stress that after buying it, they will be constantly telling themselves what a great decision it was.
- Provide audio testimonials of others endorsing your product.

## KINAESTHETIC PREFERENCE

- Your location needs comfortable chairs and suitable temperature.
- Your first physical contact will make a lasting impression – ensure that you give a good handshake.
- Your presentation needs to engage your prospect and make them feel good about your product.

- Make sure they can touch and feel the product or interact with a demonstration.

- Have them physically move around during the presentation rather than just sit in their seat.

Now that you understand the VAK meta program in more detail, it is time to learn about some of the other patterns that influence sales and communication. Whilst there really is no limit to the number of meta programs that can exist depending on creativity and originality, one of the foremost books on the subject, "Figuring Out People" by Michael Hall, identified 51 such patterns.

Rather than look into all of these, we are going to focus on those that have the potential to play a large part in our sales process, either in terms of communication styles or decision making processes.

For each of the meta programs, I will provide you with a description of the tendencies and how you might recognise the pattern in either language or behaviour. I will also give you a number of ways that you can adapt your sales process to maximise your connection with this element of your prospect.

## TOWARDS – AWAY

If you have ever been to a beach and taken a donkey ride, you will understand this meta program. The donkey has two choices; either chase after the carrot you are dangling in front of its face, or get a whack from the stick of the donkey handler. Either way, that donkey is going to go forwards.

Your prospect will either be motivated by achieving their goals and making something positive happen, or they will be driven by their desire to avoid problems and feeling as though they are missing out. Knowing which is their primary motivating force will allow you to adjust your pitch accordingly.

Whatever your product or service, there will be ways of framing it for either 'towards' or 'away from' motivation styles. If you sell insurance, you can either provide a nest egg for your family should something happen (towards) or avoid the financial catastrophe that could happen if the major household income stopped (away). Knowing which aspect to emphasise will help your close rate.

## Towards

- Move toward what they want and what they like.

- May have difficulty in recognising what should be avoided.

- Tend to play down negative consequences.

- Will tell you specifically what they want.

- Often set goals and targets.

## Sales Focus

- Use 'positive' language.

- Emphasise the benefits and positive impact of your product.

- Motivated by getting better results.

## Away From

- Avoid what they don't want or don't like.

- Easily identify problems arising in situations.

- May have trouble defining and articulating goals.

- Will tell you what they don't want.

- Make contingency plans.

## Sales Focus

- Use 'negative' language.

- Emphasise how your product will solve their problems.

- Motivated by threats and fear of loss.

See if you can identify which of the following passages has a towards preference and which is more away from.

- I really like your product. We have some pretty lofty goals and I can definitely see how what you are offering will help us in getting there. We have been discussing recently how to accelerate the process and if you can deliver on your promises, it would be great to have you on board. There are a few concerns I have, but if you can help me understand how you would be able to get around these, I am pretty confident we can get this started.

- I really like your product. We have some seriously challenging targets from management and I'm not sure we will get anywhere near without bringing in some external support. We have been discussing the challenges we had in the past with this and are pretty keen not to make the same mistakes. There are a few concerns all round, mainly because we have had our hands burnt in the past. However, I don't really see any other options at present.

## INTERNAL – EXTERNAL

This preference indicates how a person makes judgements - either from external sources, or by using their own internal standards. This is known as the frame of reference that your prospect uses for making decisions.

People with an internal reference will evaluate things based on what they think is appropriate and will stand by their own decisions. If they seek input from others, it will be to help them figure out the best possible response, either seeking to reinforce their own thoughts or they may intentionally look for a counter argument if they believe a better option exists. In the end, they will go with what they feel is the right thing to do.

Those with an external frame of reference will still make their own decisions, but will likely ask others for input and support before committing to anything. They may tend to defer authority to others who they believe more able to make the best decision in that situation. If they are in positions of power, they will likely have people that they turn to in order to help them make decisions. You will want to find these influencers if you want your prospect to make a decision in your favour.

## Internal

- Tend to rely on their own criteria, evaluations and judgements.
- Have a tendency to ignore feedback from others.
- May appear to be overconfident or arrogant.
- Possess leadership qualities and will have strong opinions.
- Know that they've done a good job based on their own subjective criteria.

## Sales Focus

- Ask them what their instincts are telling them to do.
- Reinforce their positive comments throughout the meeting and refer back to things they have said to support your argument.
- Talk about blazing trails and being recognised for the good decision.

## External

- Use external standards and feedback to develop their own opinions.
- Need feedback from others and may be swayed by others' opinions.
- May lack confidence and possess 'followership' qualities.
- Tend to draw conclusions based primarily on the other person's reactions.
- They rely on others to tell them when they've done a good job.

## Sales Focus

- Gather input from other people involved in the purchase and put forward their thoughts to support your argument.
- Ensure that all decision makers and influencers are involved.

- Reinforce what others will say when deal the is complete.

See if you can identify which of the following passages has a internal preference and which is more external.

- So we have discussed your proposal in the team meeting this morning and I think we are pretty keen to go ahead. Jonathan was really keen on that particular feature and Ben told me that your offering is a lot better than everything else on the market. We did seriously consider another couple of providers and also one that someone recommended to me as well. I'm sorry it has taken so long, but we had to make sure we had everything covered.

- Ok, so we discussed it this morning in our meeting and I am glad the team finally came around to the right decision. From what I can see, there might be a few bits we need to work on together, but you are the better solution. I am confident that over the next few months, we'll be able to make everything I have planned for the business come together.

## BIG CHUNK - SMALL CHUNK

This preference indicates the size of the "chunk" of information that a person prefers when thinking, communicating and learning. Some people prefer to deal with detailed, specific information whereas others prefer the big picture and a global overview.

*Think about this question for a moment - 'how was your weekend?'*

How would you answer this question? Would you give a detailed run down of everything that happened to you right from leaving the office on Friday night to breakfast on Monday morning? Might you instead just reply 'Yeah, it was good. You?'.

How would you feel if people replied with each of the above responses? Would the detailed response be interesting to you or overbearing? Would the overview response be fine or would you feel cheated of the details?

Make sure you give your prospect the appropriate level of information that they want and need in order to decide to do business with you.

## Small Chunk

- Want the details first before they make any decisions.

- Take time to process, as they are dealing with more information.

- Tend to perceive a task in terms of its constituent parts.

- Break down tasks into smaller, more specific and definite steps.

- May miss the overall goal of a task because they get caught in the details.

## Sales Focus

- Give access to numbers, details and spreadsheets if available.

- Introduce to the technical people in your business, especially if you are in the technology industry or similar.

- Make sure that this person is the decision maker and that there is no one else involved with more of a strategic overview.

## Big Chunk

- Need global picture first before they can put the parts in their proper place.

- Process quickly but may jump to conclusions with details.

- Focus on key points and not really interested in details.

- Tend to talk in generalities and abstract examples.

- Generally convinced by an overall concept or idea.

**Sales Focus**

- Ensure you give a good overview of the project, including what is most important about the potential deal.

- Talk more strategically rather than the how of implementation.

- Find the person in the organisation that will implement the solution and make sure you have them on board.

See if you can identify which of the following passages has a small chunk preference and which is more big chunk.

- So how exactly do you expect this to happen? What normally happens when one of your clients come on board. We used someone for this before and they just left the product with us, assuming we knew how to use it. Do you have an instruction manual that you can send us? Is there any training on how to use each of the features? We need to make sure that everyone is trained in it's use so when do you think we can get that booked in?

- Right, I think I've got it. So once you deliver the product, we'll get a manual and some training and then we'll be able to use it? Great! OK, well that all seems fine, can't wait!

## OPTIONS – PROCEDURES

Have you ever wondered what those little pamphlets are that come with electrical appliances? If so, chances are you have an options preference.

Options people do not believe in there being one right way to do things. Instead, they prefer to figure out strategies for themselves. Options people write the instruction manuals for appliances, but then ignore it and do it completely differently the next time they use it. These people tend to be more inventive in nature, creating new ideas rather than accepting the status quo.

Procedures people need to know how to do something before they start. They love paint by numbers and will make sure they stay in the lines and always paint the colours in order. They believe that if they are told to do something then this must be the 'right way'. These people make great lawyers and HR executives who need to be accurate and go 'by the book'.

## Options

- Motivated by possibility and alternatives.
- Dislikes choices being limited.
- Changes track easily and will take short-cuts if possible.
- Tends to be curious and interested in the unknown.
- Will find other applications for products and services.

## Sales Focus

- Highlight all of the potential applications of your product or service and allow the prospect to imagine themselves using.
- Ask how they would want to implement your solution with the team.
- Be prepared to be flexible from your usual sales process or product offering as you may need something more bespoke.

## Procedures

- Believe there is a 'right' way and motivated by correctness.
- Like following procedures and don't need choice.
- Compelled to complete a procedure once started.
- Tend to be more interested in what is known and what's secure.
- Difficulty in situations with no predetermined courses of action.

## Sales Focus

- Highlight the step by step process that will happen on completion.
- Let them know about the after sales support that you offer.

- Provide case studies on how other people have used your solution and how they got the most out of it.

See if you can identify which of the following passages has an options preference and which is more procedures.

- Ok, so how long after we sign the paperwork will the product get delivered? And once we have it with us, how long do you think it will take us to get up to full speed using it? We already have the staff segmented into groups for the training program and the executives are having an intensive session on the 5-step process you highlighted.

- Right, when are you getting that thing delivered? I'm thinking we get some of the staff trained first, starting with the new starters. I have another company that I want to bring in as well as this will be great for them. Oooh, what does that button do? I can't wait to get playing with all those buttons, find out what they all do.

## WHAT IS YOUR PREFERENCE?

Be careful not to apply your preferences to your sales pitch too much. This is easier said than done, but the first step to improving is to be aware of the challenge. In fact, if you read through this book, you will probably get a good idea of what my preferences are.

You do not need to exclusively communicate using your prospect's preferences as this may seem unnatural and disjointed. However, the more flexibility you have, the less resistance you will encounter.

If you are facing challenges communicating with a particular prospect, adjusting your language patterns to fit their preferences might be a good idea.

*"Personally I am very fond of strawberries and cream, but I have found that for some strange reason, fish prefer worms. So when I went fishing, I didn't think about what I wanted. I thought about what they wanted. I didn't bait the hook with strawberries and cream. Rather, I dangled a worm or grasshopper in front of the fish and said: "Wouldn't you like to have that?"*

*Why not use the same common sense when fishing for people?"*

- **Dale Carnegie**

## WARNING - MIS-MATCHERS

Although this is a meta program in it's own right, I want to warn you of a small section of the population that have the potential to throw you off track. These people are particularly programmed to spot differences and they arrange their life to get as many differences as they possible can.

This includes differences of opinion, in appearance, in behaviour. Anything they can do to be different to you they will do... ANYTHING!

Have you ever been in a situation with a prospect and it doesn't matter what you do, you just cant get into rapport? Mis-matcher!

Have you ever told that joke you tell all your prospects and they all laugh but this person just sat there cold as ice? Mis-matcher!

Have you ever tried to match body language and yet every move you make your prospect immediately shifts too? Mis-matcher!

Mis-matchers are vital to society as they are the devils advocate. They slow the creators down and ensure that ideas make sense, that everything is in place, that all the alternatives have been considered before proceeding.

Selling to them, however, can be a bit of a nightmare! It will seem like everything you try has no effect and you leave the meeting completely dejected. However, for some reason, you get back and there is an email waiting confirming the deal and stating how much they enjoyed the meeting. What the...?

Just be aware that there are people out there that will do everything they can to be different to you. When you meet these people, stay strong and stick to your plan. Don't let them throw you off track. Don't chase after them to get the responses you are looking for. Instead, just be confident in yourself and do your thing... you'll be surprised at the outcome!

Next Level Persuasion is about developing relationships with your clients, starting from your first encounter and developing as you continue to work together. Whilst other salespeople are still out there matching and mirroring body language and trying to square-peg their interests with their prospect, you now understand what rapport really is and how to develop it at a deeper level. Relationships don't have to be overly friendly, but instead should be built on a mutual trust and respect for each other which is developed through truly understanding the person in front of you.

**Here are some of the main points to take away from this chapter.**

- Become a master at developing rapport but remember there comes a time to lead. You cannot sell without rapport, but you also cannot sell if you stay on your prospect's agenda. Take control of the conversation and learn how to bring your prospect round to your way of thinking.

- Develop your awareness and notice what is happening behind your prospect's words. Watch how they move their body. Notice changes in their tonality and speech. In the same way as you give off unconscious signals, you need to be able to read them on the people you meet.

- Don't settle for superficial rapport. Your best friend knows all of your darkest secrets and whilst you do not need to go to this level, you do need to know more about your prospect than what they had for lunch. Ask more probing questions as your relationship begins to develop.

- Understand that we all have different preferences and ways we like to communicate. Even though we use the same language, we each listen for different information, process it differently and then speak with subtle idiosyncrasies. Know thyself and recognise your own tendencies first.

# CHAPTER 7
# EDUCATING

| OPENING | CONNECTING | EDUCATING | MOTIVATING | COMMITTING |
|---------|------------|-----------|------------|------------|

| PREPARING |
|-----------|

| PURPOSE |
|---------|

*"It usually takes me more than three weeks to prepare a good impromptu speech."*

**- Mark Twain**

*"I'm a great believer that any tool that enhances communication has profound effects in terms of how people can learn from each other, and how they can achieve the kind of freedoms that they're interested in."*

**- Bill Gates**

Remember our definition of sales? At the end of your sales meeting, your prospect is going to have to make a decision, and of course we are hoping that the decision they make is to buy our product or service.

*Sales is getting someone to do something*

*that you want them to do,*

*whether they realize they want to do it yet or not.*

Take a moment and think back to the last decision you made. What was the process you went through when it came to finally deciding and committing to that action?

For most of us, we weigh up the pros and cons of each decision based on what we know about the relevant consequences and then compare that to the amount of investment required. If the price is right and the benefits add up, then there is a good chance that is the decision we will make.

In our Educating phase of selling, we need to position ourselves and our product in such a way that by the end of the process, we are the obvious choice. However, we need to do it in a particular way.

Have you ever been in a situation where you feel as though you have no choice, and that the only thing you can do is the one option you have in front of you? How do you feel in those kinds of situations?

Personally, I prefer choice and variety as the opposite makes me unsure of whether I am making the right decision. If I only have one choice, I don't have anything to compare against so how do I know how good the deal is in front of me? Could I have bought something better for my situation or could I have got the same deal for a better price? Because I only have the one option in front of me, it actually makes me less likely to buy.

In the old world of sales, the close was all about reducing the number of options. In fact, the classic closing technique of 'double-bind' reduced all options down to just two, but in reality both options involved buying the product. Salespeople applied this pattern in every situation possible.

*"I'm in your area next week, which would you prefer - Tuesday morning or Wednesday afternoon?"*

*"Would you prefer the upgraded ticket or just the standard package?"*

*"Do you want me to come round weekly or monthly?"*

As consumers became aware of sales techniques, one of the first realisations was that there was in fact a third option, and that was to say no entirely. The double bind should have been retired a long time ago but as you know, old habits die hard! (In fact, you'll be learning how to use double binds properly later in the book.)

The problem with the double bind is that it removed the freedom of choice from the prospect. Without the ability to choose a different option, our prospects tend to be hesitant to agree to make the decision to buy.

However, we also know that if we give our prospects too much choice, they also tend to hesitate. If we open the doors up completely, a form of analysis paralysis can arise, with so many options making decisions difficult. Any element of confusion will stall a sale, with your prospect likely needing to think about things until they have absolute clarity in their mind. And do you think they will ever get around to think about it? Unlikely.

So what is the answer?

The answer lies in Educating our prospects in a way that seems to give them all the choice they need but which narrows the obvious choice down to your solution. We need to educate them as to all of the different ways to solve their particular problem, but then highlight the potential pitfalls in working with any of the other possible solutions. If you narrow down the options enough, the only sensible decision is to work with you.

Your challenge is to educate in a way which does not feel to the prospect as though you are influencing them directly. If you simply tell your client all of the problems associated with your competitors, there will be a lot of resistance. Instead of telling them, you need to find a way that helps them come to that realisation themselves.

---

I'll give you a clue... it involves questions!

The educating element of the Next Level Persuasion process involves asking questions that can help you to understand your prospect's current model of the world while positioning yourself and your product in the appropriate way. Let's start off by looking at some of the general linguistic patterns first before understanding how to put these together in a complete sales process.

# POWERFUL COMMUNICATION PATTERNS

As suggested by the 'L' in NLP, there are a number of linguistic patterns that, once learned and practiced, can help to make you a more powerful communicator. As with all of the concepts of NLP, these are linguistic constructs that you already use, and yet drawing your attention to them will help you use them by design, rather than by accident.

Many of these linguistic patterns were discovered during the modelling of therapists such as Virginia Satir, Fritz Perls and Milton Erickson during the initial creation of NLP. These therapists were all interested in one thing - changing the thought patterns and action of their clients.

By incorporating these language patterns into your sales process, you will become a masterful communicator and powerful influencer. Each pattern has a wide range of applications, but we cannot explain every possible use. However, I will give situational examples where suitable.

### LEVELS OF ABSTRACTION - CHUNKING UP & CHUNKING DOWN

During conversations, we have a tendency to move between different levels of detail or abstraction. Salespeople need to know how and when to ask detail-related questions, and when it may be useful to discuss things at a higher level. This questioning model can be used to help get greater clarity in the information you are giving and receiving, and can also be a useful tool in objection handling and reframing.

'Chunking' is the NLP term for moving the conversation up or down the levels of abstraction. Chunking up makes things more abstract and chunking down moves things back down into the detail. To do this, you need to know these questions:

Chunking Up:
*What is this an example of?*
*For what purpose?*
*What is the intention?*

Chunking Down:
*What is an example of this?*
*What specifically?*
*What sort of?*

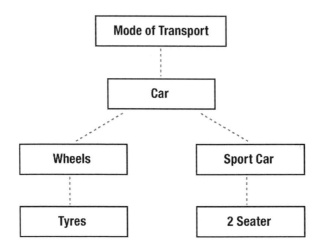

Chunking down is vital for ensuring the details of a project are discovered. Let's say you sell photocopiers for example, and you have agreed a sale. Which photocopier do you provide? In this instance, you need to know how many pages they print per day? Does the prospect print in colour? How is the office networked? Missing the detail will mean that you will be unlikely to provide the best possible product.

Chunking up allows you to understand the motivation behind a purchase. Asking the purpose behind buying something will lead you into the values of your prospect and you will discover the buying motives. It also helps open the conversation in terms of other opportunities to achieve the same outcome.

Let's say you don't offer the exact service your prospect is looking for. Do you lose the opportunity, or do you try and switch the prospect round to your way of thinking? To switch the customer, firstly chunk up to understand the reasons behind the potential purchase, and then chunk back down to find other alternatives that meet this requirement.

For example, you are a hotel and get an enquiry for a location 1 mile away. If you ask the chunking up question, ask why they want that particular area, you discover that it is because the prospect wants to have a day out in that area. What are other ways to meet this need? Perhaps you could offer a free shuttle. Perhaps you have transport links right outside your hotel. If your prospect is happy to take one of these options, you have yourself a deal you would otherwise have missed out on.

Later on, you will discover how to chunk laterally to help overcome objections. For now, ensure that you understand how to chunk up and down to get the right level of detail or abstraction with your prospect.

## PRESUPPOSITIONS

A presupposition is 'a thing tacitly assumed beforehand at the beginning of a line of argument or course of action'. In linguistics, presuppositions are clauses in a phrase that have to be accepted for the sentence to make sense.

Salespeople can use presuppositions in their conversation and questions to force their prospects to accept elements that he or she does not want questioned. The truly excellent sales person can use these linguistic patterns to really influence his or her prospect in to associating their needs to a particular solution or product. Notice the difference in the two following statements.

1. How might you implement a solution?
2. How would you implement our solution?

Did you spot the difference? In this case there are two presuppositions in the second question. In the first sentence, there is doubt and lack of ownership of the solution. In the second sentence, the presuppositions are that they are going to take a solution, and secondly that it belongs to the salesperson's company.

*How can you use presuppositions in your questioning?*
(Presupposition that you can.)

*How much better will your questions be when you begin to use presuppositions?*
(Presupposition your questions will be better and you will begin.)

*What improvement in your sales will these questions have?*
(Presupposition of an improvement.)

Many sales people use these techniques unconsciously and sporadically. The best salespeople always make use of presuppositions when it is appropriate to do so.

Be aware that if you use a presupposition and your prospect does not accept it, you may need to follow up with a different question that leaves it a little more open. For example, the old 'double bind' closing technique used presuppositions:

*I'm in your area next week. Which day do you prefer for our meeting: Tuesday or Thursday?*

(Presupposition the prospect wants to meet you.)

However, now if you ask that question to any prospect, the chances are they will laugh in your face unless they have actually bought into the idea of having a meeting with you.

Use presuppositions well and you will be able to ask some very powerful questions that will lead your prospects exactly where you want them to go.

# THE META MODEL

*"The map is not the territory."*

**- Alfred Korzybski**

Have you ever been in a meeting with a client and it seems that nothing they say makes any sense? They seem to be arguing every point with you and continually going around the houses, never getting to the actual root cause of their point of view. Infuriatingly you attempt to keep up with their rant but they eventually get to a point where they have frustrated themselves to the point of not wanting to buy.

If this has ever happened to you, the chances are that your prospect does not actually know how to explain the problem with language. They know how it feels instinctively, but getting that across to someone else is not as easy. This is where you need to understand the meta model of questioning.

The Meta Model communication patterns are used to improve the specificity and accuracy of the information your prospect is giving you. The closer the map reflects the territory, the more useful the map becomes. By asking the selected questions you will discover below, you will be able to assist your prospect in giving you the information you require to help proceed the sale.

## HOW OUR BRAIN PROCESSES SENSORY INFORMATION

Our minds are being bombarded with more information than we are able to consciously handle each and every second. Think about all of your senses and what is going on around you at this exact moment. If you had to be aware of every single aspect of your environment, you simply would not be able to function.

In order to cope, our brain has three protective mechanisms that help us make sense of all the information. You will hopefully recognise these from the Connecting part of the book.

These are:    *Deletion*    *Distortion*    *Generalisation*

---

Deletion is when our conscious mind simply omits certain information which it deems unnecessary for a given situation. We are constantly processing information through our five senses, but unless I draw your attention to something, the chances are you are only aware of a small amount of what is actually happening.

For example, no doubt you are aware of your sight right now as you are reading this. But are you aware of the feeling of your clothes against your skin? Can you hear those noises in the distance? Do you notice the temperature of the skin on the back of your hands?

This on its own is not a problem as long as your mind does not delete the important information (don't worry, it wont). The challenges come when you try and recall the specific information but because you have deleted some of it on the way in, it doesn't necessarily come out as accurately as it could.

Distortion is where we bend and twist what we experience to make it fit our model of the world. For example, if you see a prospect has their arms crossed, what does that mean? In truth, it doesn't mean anything, but we have a tendency to try and ascribe meaning based on experiences and beliefs we may have. Distortion helps us make sense of situations where we have incomplete information of the situation.

Nominalisation is one way that distortion occurs in our language systems. In our minds, we change an ongoing process into an event with a beginning and an end. This allows us to compartmentalise complex processes into a larger concept that is more simple for us to consider. Words such as 'relationship', 'decision' and 'management' are all examples of nominalisations.

Generalisations happen when we try and categorise the world and group things together or when we adopt beliefs about the world. When we create groups, it means we have less information to sort through when trying to interpret our senses. For example, if we assume all chairs have 4 legs, a back and a flat seating area, then any time we see something similar, we assume it is safe to use as a chair.

However, when we generalise, this takes away the chance for anomalies or exceptions to the rule. For example, if we have the generalisation 'all farmers drive combine harvesters!' and we meet a farmer, what do you assume about their preferred means of travel? If you see a combine harvester, what do you assume about the owner? This may be a frivolous example, but I am sure you can imagine the impact generalisations have on life.

## DELETIONS, DISTORTIONS AND GENERALISATIONS IN LANGUAGE

The key principle of the meta model is the NLP presupposition that 'the map is not the territory', a concept encapsulated by Alfred Korzybski who developed the theory of general semantics. (This presupposition was not included in the list earlier in the book as it is not hugely sales related, but is important to consider here.) This presupposition suggests that no matter how well you describe something linguistically, you can never quite get across the whole picture.

The meta model therefore attempts to close the gap between the map and the territory, or in sales, the information you are being given and the real situation. We will explore 10 key linguistic patterns of the meta model below, and give sales examples for each pattern.

**Beware** - if you get really good at using these questions, it can appear that you are a great arguer. Make sure that you use softening language if necessary to avoid any potential confrontations.

## 10 META MODEL CONCEPTS

| | |
|---|---|
| Mind Reading | Universal Quantifiers |
| Lost Performative | Modal Operators |
| Cause-Effect | Nominalisations |
| Complex Equivalence | Unspecified Verbs |
| Presuppositions | Comparative Deletions |

## 1 - MIND READING

These linguistic patterns are where your prospect assumes to know the internal thoughts, feelings or intentions of another person. There may be no factual basis or information, so the prospect must be imagining what he or she thinks is happening.

*Examples:*
He's upset with me!
I know what you want!

*Responses:*
How do you know he's upset with you?
How do you know what I want?

## 2 - LOST PERFORMATIVE

These patterns are value judgements, rules and beliefs where the source of the assertion is missing. They often involve generic statements or common preconceptions.

*Examples:*
Spending money on advertising is risky!
Men don't buy beauty products!

*Responses:*
Who says it is risky?
According to whom?
How do you know men don't buy them?

## 3 - CAUSE-EFFECT

These patterns involve the belief that one person's action can cause another person's reaction. This goes against the idea that people have the ability to choose their reaction to events and assumes a causal connection.

*Examples:*
Salespeople make me mad!
Spending my boss' money makes me nervous!

*Responses:*
How, specifically, do sales people make you mad?
Why does that cause you to choose to feel that way!

## 4 - COMPLEX EQUIVALENCE

This pattern brings two unrelated statements together to give the impression they have the same meaning. These patterns often contain the clause 'that means' in between two statements.

*Example:*
You're late for this meeting. You don't care about my business.
You didn't call us back. You are obviously too busy for us.

*Responses:*
How does being late mean I don't care?

Have you ever been on time for something that you didn't care about?

How specifically does me not calling mean I am too busy?

## 5 - PRESUPPOSITIONS

These are phrases that include assumptions that have to be believed for the sentence to make sense. We can use these to our advantage in our questions, and we also need to recognise them when prospects use them in conversation.

*Examples:*
We aren't going to do anything until March!
We haven't tried anything since the last time we used one!

*Responses:*
So you have decided to take action on this project then?
You have tried this product before then?

## 6 - UNIVERSAL QUANTIFIERS

This pattern involves statements that include universal generalisations such as all, every or never. The response needs to be to challenge the universality of the claim.

*Examples:*
All salespeople are conmen!
We always chose the wrong providers!

*Responses:*
ALL salespeople?
Have you ever made a good choice?

## 7 - MODAL OPERATORS

These are words that imply rules or conditions for behaviour - should, must, can't. The two modal operators are those of possibility and necessity implying things either can be done or need to be done.

*Examples:*
There is no way that can be done!
You have to make it work like this!

*Responses:*
What would happen if it could?
What would happen if we did? Didn't?

## 8 - NOMINALISATIONS

These are process words with the time element removed and have therefore been reduced to a noun. A nominalisation is a noun that is not actually an item. If you want to check whether a noun is a nominalisation, ask yourself the question 'can I put this in a wheelbarrow?'. Nominalisations are nouns that aren't actually tangible.

*Examples:*
Relationships are difficult!
We need better management!

*Responses:*
What part of your relationship specifically is challenging?
How can management improve their processes?

## 9 - UNSPECIFIED VERBS

These are verbs that delete the specifics of the process itself, rather than giving the full sentence with all the information required for it to make sense.

*Examples:*
He tries too hard!
They want me to do it!

*Responses:*
How, specifically?
Want you to do what exactly?

## 10 - COMPARATIVE DELETIONS

This pattern involves statements where the standard of comparison is left out, especially involving phrases like 'more than' or 'less than'.

*Examples:*
I want a better service provider!
We need faster response times!

*Responses:*
Better than whom?
Faster than what?
Compared to whom, what?

Now you understand the meta-model questions, you will become excellent at argumentation. You will literally be able to pull apart the argument of someone until they have nowhere else to run. You have all the weapons you require to destroy someone verbally.

*"You can't win an argument. You can't because if you lose it, you lose it; and if you win it, you lose it."*

**- Dale Carnegie**

However, doing that in a sales situation is probably not the best course of action. Therefore, you need to deliver the responses in a subtle, sympathetic style rather than the direct, challenging way. For example:

*We need faster response times!*

(Direct response) *Faster than what?*

(Indirect response) *I'm curious, you say you want faster response times. What are you comparing this to? Have you experienced a problem with response times in the past?*

It is important to know what to say when faced with a meta-model violation, and it is vital that you deliver this in a way that helps you maintain rapport with your prospect. Master these questioning responses and you will be able to guide your sales conversation in whatever direction you wish to take it.

## HYPNOTIC PATTERNS

The opposite of the specificity of the meta model is the abstract nature of the hypnotic language patterns. Where the meta model helps you get more information in terms of details, hypnosis allows you to direct the thoughts of your prospect

Hypnotic patterns are used clinically to help clients create new imagery and change thought patterns to be more beneficial. Salespeople can use these patterns to bring prospects round to their way of thinking as well as helping to bring about certain emotional responses which assist in closing the sale.

Each of the meta model patterns can be reversed in order to create hypnotic statements and questions, and there are a number of unique patterns that can also be used.

## MIND READ

Using mind reads allows you to develop a greater level of rapport through understanding, assuming you get things right. Prospects want to know that you have a deep understanding of their situation before they will start to trust you. By making statements that are true for the prospect, you will be able to generate rapport as well as seem like an expert in selling the product or service you have.

*I know you are probably a little nervous about working with someone new on this project...*

*I know what you are thinking about this product...*

## TAG QUESTIONS

If you ever find that you have to talk for an extended period of time, there is a danger of disconnecting and breaking rapport with your prospect. Instead of just continuing to talk, it would be a good idea to keep your prospect involved, wouldn't it? This way, even though they are not actually responding, it still feels like they are part of the conversation, doesn't it? This is what tag questions allow you to do. They imply the answer, but don't actually require a response.

*It will be great when you start using this, won't it!*

*This option is far better than the other, isn't it!*

## DOUBLE BIND

Although this technique has been used in the past as a closing technique and has become frowned upon, it can still be used as a linguistic pattern. A double bind suggests a number of options, but in reality, any and all options lead to the situation that the salesperson desires.

*So we can get this started today, or we can leave it until the end of the month if you prefer?*

*Whether you realise you need this product immediately or later, as soon as you begin to use it, you will forget what life was like without it.*

## EXTENDED QUOTE

Salespeople, unfortunately, still have a reputation for saying anything just to get a sale. This means that anything a salesperson says is likely to be met with a certain amount of apprehension. Using extended quotes, that is referring to something that someone else said, can help get around that challenge. Extended quotes can include testimonials and also any research or data you may have for your product or service.

*I overheard a conversation the other day where someone was saying how useful this product had been for her family.*

*I was at a business seminar the other day and the speaker was saying how this service was going to be the revolution of the future.*

## AMBIGUITY

The two major ambiguities that are useful for a salesperson are Phonological and Syntactic. Phonological ambiguity uses words that sound the same with the same meaning, such as 'there', 'they're' and 'their'. Syntactic ambiguity makes the punctuation unclear, leaving room for the sentence to be interpreted in more than one way.

*You are here and you hear what I'm saying about this, can't you?*

*So now when would be a good time to start?*

## SELECTIONAL RESTRICTIONAL VIOLATION

This is potentially the most complicated name for a linguistic pattern ever. It describes the way we ascribe attributes to something that shouldn't have those qualities. Often times it is used to give human characteristics to inanimate objects.

*Can you hear that car calling you?*

*Just feel the sofa wrapping its arms around you!*

## ASSOCIATED VS DISSOCIATED

As we know, decisions are made emotionally and then that choice is justified with logic. With this in mind, we need to know how to get people to feel emotional, and conversely, when it is appropriate to take the emotion out of the conversation.

We have all had that experience of watching a scary movie and jumping as the monster/alien/bad guy (which is your favourite?) creeps out of the dark right behind the star of the movie, but which do you think is scarier: watching the movie, or being the person who is being chased? I'm sure you are glad that you are the one with the popcorn rather than the person on screen in those situations.

This is the difference between associated and dissociated. A person who is associated is in the picture, they are involved and things are happening directly to them. Someone who is dissociated by contrast is detached, an observer who may or may not have a vested interest in the situation.

If we are going to get people to feel emotion, we need to use associated language. To do this, you need to make sure the person is involved and you do that by directing their imagination accordingly.

- How do you feel when your employees act in that way?

- What will this solution mean regarding time with your family?

- Now, what are you going to do about this problem?

With association, get people to imagine themselves in the picture, either by asking them to feel something, imagine a scenario or by changing the timeline aspect and bringing it into the present moment. This way, what you are getting them to associate to will seem more real and have a greater emotional impact.

In NLP, we use dissociative language to help people feel less emotional about a given situation. For example, if you are trying to deal with someone's phobia, it would probably be useful for them not to freak out every time you mention the thing they are scared of. In this example, we would actually put someone in a cinema and get them to watch themselves on the big screen. You can even move them to the projection box and get them to watch themselves watching themselves on the big screen if you need to get them really dissociated.

In sales, dissociation can be useful for objections, as there is normally an element of emotion around this subject. Perceptual positions is one objection handling method that we have discussed, and this is an example of taking people out of themselves and thereby removing the emotion of the situation.

- If you had to do this over, what kind of advice would you give yourself?

- What would your mentor recommend that you do?

- Who is someone that is successful? How did they do it?

Take the person out of the equation, get them to imagine themselves as someone else, or change the time perspective to a point where they can look objectively at the situation. Each of these will help reduce the emotional intensity of a conversation.


## QUESTIONING MODELS

*"Judge a man by his questions rather than by his answers."*
**- Voltaire**


*"Questions are great, but only if you know the answers. If you ask questions and the answers surprise you, you look silly. "*
**- Laurell K. Hamilton**

Talk less, listen more. Great advice for all sales people.

I am resisting writing a number of sales cliches at this point, particularly those about the ratios between ears and mouths. However, the fact remains that, especially at the beginning of a sales meeting, your job is to get your prospect to talk. There are two ways to achieve this. The first involves sitting there quietly until the client says something to break the awkward silence (not advisable). The second, and probably more effective strategy is to ask a question.

So, what questions do you ask?

Good question! (Remember to say this if you find yourself getting asked a tricky question. It buys you just about enough time to come up with a sensible answer!)

In this section, we are going to cover the various types of questions you can ask, as well as the order and structure of your questions. All of your questions should be designed to take the conversation towards the final question which will always be:

*"So, do we have a deal?"*

Or at least something along those lines. However, there are a number of different ways to get there.

**We are going to look at two major models for questioning:**

- The SCORE Model
- The Neurological Levels Model

Both of these models will give us an outline for the type of questions we need to ask and are designed in a way that will get your prospect to a point where they want you to close them.

Before we look into detail at these models however, we need to learn about the two different types of fundamental questions.

## 2 TYPES OF QUESTION

In the world of communication, there are many different types of question; open, closed, presuppositions, assumptive, leading, rhetorical, multi-choice, provocative, hypothetical, divergent, irreverent. These styles of questions can be combined to make more complex style questions and each can be asked in a number of ways.

In sales, we only ever really ask one of two fundamental types of question.

• Discovery

• Positioning

## DISCOVERY

A discovery question is where you are genuinely looking to find out information from your prospect. Typically an open style question, you are inviting your prospect to tell you more about a particular aspect of the SCORE model. For example, you might want to know about their current situation in the Symptom section, so you would ask:

• What problems have you been experiencing recently?

• How have the latest changes impacted you and your business?

Each of these questions will allow you to learn more than you previously knew about your prospect. You ask these questions to open up different aspects of the conversation and to attempt to uncover particular angles you can later discuss with your prospect.

Asking open questions can be risky though if you do not know the answer. In general, you should ask discovery questions towards the beginning of your sales interaction, whilst you are still building rapport and trying to get more of an understanding about your prospect.

## POSITIONING

Once you have built up a strong client profile, you should begin to ask questions that you know the answer to. These are your positioning questions. By asking positioning questions, you are directing and guiding the thoughts of your prospect in the direction you want them to go. Many of these questions will include presuppositions.

For example, let's say your product has a particular unique selling point. How do you get your prospect to understand the benefit of the unique selling point to their situation? Well, you could tell them how great it is, but as you already know, telling them is not going to get your prospect to buy into the idea. Ideally, you want them to tell you the benefits so that they have to visualise the solution. Which of the following two questions do you think would accomplish this most effectively?

- What do you think the most important features of this particular product should be?

- How would you make the most of this unique selling point when you start using this product?

With the first question, you are hoping that your prospect mentions one of your features so that you can respond positively to their request. However, what if they do not mention any of your features right from the start? This is often where sales people will chase the prospect with direct questions that are obviously about the features that their product can offer.

Instead, the second question positions your product and unique selling point in your prospect's mind so that they are forced to consider using your product. The truth is you know exactly how your USP will be useful to your prospect, so you are not asking this question to get an answer. Instead, this positioning question uses presuppositions to force your prospect to see things in the way you want them to be seen.

# QUESTIONING MODEL - SCORE MODEL

Robert Dilts and Todd Epstein devised the SCORE model in 1987 as a process for defining problems and designing interventions. It added extra layers to the symptom, outcome, process model that was being used in NLP at that particular time.

As salespeople, our goal is to help prospects identify the problems they are currently facing and help them close this gap by suggesting a solution or intervention. This makes the SCORE model perfect as a sales questioning model, and turns salespeople into coaches that are helping people to buy their solution.

The SCORE model gives a 5-step framework that allows you to design a series of questions that allow prospects to make a decision to change that ideally involves your product or service. It is not about telling a prospect how to behave, instead it is about getting them to realise what is important to them and facilitating their new behaviours to achieve their goals.

Too often, salespeople try and convince their prospects that a particular product or service is superior, and whilst this may work, it is not the most ecological sales methodology. Instead of pushing our product, our goal with the SCORE model is the following 5 steps:

1.  Highlight a particular problem or gap;

2.  Understand rationale behind current situation;

3.  Gain clarity on the nature of the ideal situation;

4.  Identify potential solutions for the problem;

5.  Raise motivation to encourage immediate action.

Each of these statements ties into one of the 5 steps of the SCORE process, and will form the basis of our questioning model. Lets explore the 5 steps further.

## S - SYMPTOM

The symptom is the current situation and presenting problem. This is the reason you are talking to your prospect and the challenge they are particularly looking to remedy. The better you understand their current situation, the more likely you will be able to find opportunities for your product or service to add value.

At this point, you may be looking for certain information about the business or the individual you are facing, and may have a certain amount of basic information you need to get. However, I would be very careful to enter into this stage looking to 'fact find'. Although this is often an important part of the sale, you are still at the early stage of the sales process and developing rapport is key. If you then pull out a 100-question tick sheet, you risk breaking this rapport and boring your prospect. Instead, where possible, do the research ahead of the sales meeting. Find out as much information as you can prior to sitting down and having this conversation. This will do two things:

- Help build and develop rapport in the early stages of the meeting

- Demonstrate your preparation for the meeting and how important this prospect is to you

If you know a particular demographic well or a particular business vertical, you may be able to mind read a lot of this information. Then, rather than asking it as a question, make it a statement. This is an excellent way to demonstrate expertise and credibility to your prospect.

**Suggested Symptom questions can include:**
- What is the problem you are having with this department?
- What changes are you looking to make in your business?
- What is wrong with your current setup?

Once you have identified the existing situation, you need to understand why there has not been any change to date.

**Note** - Often, your prospect will not realise he or she has a problem. Your job as a salesperson is then to highlight the problem that they are not yet aware of. This is probably why people don't like salespeople, because they find out about all these problems that they never knew existed (Ignorance is bliss after all!).

## C - CAUSE OR CHALLENGE

The Cause or Challenge is what is holding your prospect back and will give you an idea as to why they have not already solved the problem you have highlighted. These questions are a little more probing for your prospect, and so be sure to maintain rapport and frame your questions appropriately.

For example, if you put a business owner on the spot and ask them why they have not moved with technology, you are likely to get a list of excuses and justifications. No one likes having to justify their previous actions, especially if your solution eventually sounds obvious, so find a way to let your prospect save face if this is the case. Reassure them that they are not the only person who has been in this situation.

You may also uncover a range of beliefs, many of which may be limiting, that you will need to address during your sales process. For example, take the below interchange:

**S** - Why haven't you changed this before?

**P** - I just don't think we have the resources internally to manage it!

In this situation, you need to address the limiting belief of resources. If you do not, this will become a major objection at the end of the sale.

**Examples of Cause / Challenge questions are:**
- Why have you not already changed this?
- What has held you back in the past?
- What do you think is causing this problem?

---

## O - OUTCOME

Helping your prospect develop a clear Outcome is your opportunity to paint a positive picture. Until now, it has been about problems and excuses, and now you are turning the tables and suggesting that there is a way out of their current mire.

This is your prospects opportunity to be creative and start asking for what they want and potentially identify elements they will no longer stand for. Facilitate your prospect through a 'blue sky thinking' process whereby they get to tell you their ideal situation, what would make things better than they could possibly imagine.

At the same time as facilitating this thought process, you want to start asking questions that lead prospects to understand the benefits of your product or service. For example, if your unique selling point is delivered in less than 24 hours, which of the following questions would be more useful?

• Have you thought about the delivery timescales you would expect?

• What would it mean to have delivery in less than 24 hours?

Asking the second question guides the prospect's thoughts towards the benefit of your product. You are not pitching at this point. I repeat, you are not pitching your product or service. You are simply highlighting an area where your prospect might be able to get a better service than they are currently getting.

These questions will help you start framing your pitch in your head so be sure to take lots of notes on this section particularly. This is especially true if you are selling a technically detailed product. Your prospect will be giving you lots of information that will assist you in putting together a great value pitch for your offering.

(Note - there is nothing worse than premature sales. Avoid the temptation to talk about your product or service at this point. You need to build the excitement and tension before revealing everything you have to offer.)

**Examples of Outcome questions are:**

- What would be your ideal situation?
- Can you tell me your dream service?
- What do you really want to get out of this purchase?

> **Note** - Remember our PURPLE acronym from the well formed outcomes we discussed earlier in the book? These would be useful here!

## R - RESOURCE

The resource is the bridge for the gap. If you have got the prospect clear on where they want to be using your outcome-related questions, then the gap should be evident. Hopefully you have also positioned your questions in a way so that the obvious choice for closing the gap is a product or service that you provide. Your product or service should act as the bridge from where they currently are to where they want to be.

In some cases, you may want to get your prospect to think of alternative means of solving the problem by asking a question such as:

- *"What ways can you think of that will help us achieve those outcomes together?"*
- *"What are all the options we have of closing the gap between where we are right now and where we want to get to?"*

Once you have created this list, you need to make sure you position your product or service as the best possible option.

However, rarely do you want to just give one option as this may seem to be an overt sales technique. Instead, take this opportunity to reinforce the strengths of your product by contrasting how other solutions would produce ineffective results.

For example, you are selling a product or service, and with your great questioning you have created a huge gap for your prospect that they know they need to fill. Instead of just asking for the sale there and then (you can definitely try, but you might find that although they are motivated, they may not be educated enough yet to make a good decision), this is your opportunity to teach your prospect why they should be choosing you over everyone else. So instead of asking them what they want to do, limit the choices down to three and then get them to choose from those.

Maybe the choices in this case are:

- Prospect does it themselves (possible in most service-related industries)

- Prospect buys a mid-range priced alternative

- Prospect buys the premium product or service

Where do YOU and your business fit on this list of options?

When educating your prospect, always leave your option until last to discuss it so that it seems like a logical choice and it is also freshest in your prospect's mind when you ask for the deal.

For example, let's say I am selling the mid-priced option, I might say something like this:

> *"So now you understand the challenges of running something like this yourself, and you also know the kind of fees you could end up paying if you decide to go with one of the larger companies, I guess what would be useful for you would be someone that can provide the services of the big companies but closer to the price of the DIY version, right?"*

If you think about how I positioned this middle of the road option, it would be easy to do the same for the low-cost or premium versions. Think about how you could position your product or service in a similar way to this.

What does your prospect need to close the gap from where they are right now to where they want to be? This is ideally where your product or service fits in.

## E - EFFECT

The effect questions allow you to really tap into the values and emotional elements behind the purchase. In this section, in contrast to the outcome questions that are targeted at short-term goals for this particular purchase, the effect questions look more at the longer-term perspective and wider implications of the decision.

With effect questions, we are looking to truly understand the values and motivation behind a particular purchase. Remember, ALL buying decisions are made emotionally and then backed up with logic, so if we do not know our buyers driving factors, we will not really know what they want to buy.

*People don't want to buy a drill, they want to buy the hole in the wall!*

The purchase decision your prospect is looking to make is likely a means to a particular end, and that end is going to reflect , in most cases, one of their core values. The only reason they are considering your product or service is because they believe it may be a means to that end. The effect section of questions allows you to uncover that ends value, but also then add an element of motivation by exploring the other side of the coin of inaction or poor decision, which I call the Not-Effect question.

I remember meeting a dentist once that was looking into a marketing solution for the practice she managed with her husband. She told me how they were now having to pay for the entire building as some of the tenants that had been renting rooms from her had recently moved on, at that they had also recently spent a small fortune on developing one of the treatment rooms. I also found out that her husband was doing all of the treatments himself. I also found out that she had a Porsche sat in the garage which they were both too busy to drive!

In this situation, the end goal or effect of the marketing plan was to develop a busy practice with multiple dentists and hygienists. This situation would take the pressure off her husband from having to earn all of the money required to keep the practice running and give them back some time. When it got to closing the deal and pitching my solution, I knew exactly what I had to remind her about in order to get the emotional connection necessary for her to want to buy.

**Some great examples of Effect questions could be:**
- What will this purchase allow you to go on and do?
- How else will this decision impact the business and what will that mean to you?
- What will this product mean to you personally?

The Not-Effect is a little reminder of the cost of inaction, which we cover in the objection handling formula section. Remember, pain can be used as a great motivator, especially when you want someone to take action now rather than in the future which is the goal of most salespeople, no matter how long your sales cycle. These questions require that your prospect considers not acting at all, or indeed takes the wrong sort of action. You need good levels of rapport and sincerity to ask these questions without upsetting your client so make sure you practice these in advance.

Some companies and products use the not-effect style of questioning a lot, using away-from motivation as the key driver to take action. Anyone that has ever sold insurance or retirement investments will be very *au fait* with this style of questioning and suggestion.

You have a couple of options with your not-effect questions depending on how confrontational you need to be with your client to motivate them. Firstly, you can ask the full question and encourage a response from your prospect. This gets them to associate to the situation in detail and truly consider the implications of not buying your product or service.

- Tell me, what would happen if you didn't start using this service before the end of the year?

- How do you think the team would feel if you hadn't brought in this resource to help them all?

The other option is to use softening language and a tag question in order to elicit an affirmative response without having to go into too much depth with the thoughts. This way is less likely to break rapport as much and allows you to maintain a positive flow in the conversation.

- And of course, you know I don't need to remind you of what happens to the business if we don't review the marketing, do I?
- I hope you aren't still thinking you can do this on your own, are you?

Choose the not-effect question that both suits your type of selling approach as well as your prospect's preferences.

## SCORE QUESTIONS

Now you understand the SCORE model and the various stages of questioning that you need to move people through in order to close a sale, it is time for you to write out some high quality questions that you can use in your next meeting.

Think about DISCOVERY and POSITIONING style questions and how each can be used at the various stages of questioning. How can you build in PRESUPPOSITIONS as well to help with the positioning aspect of your questions.

In your meetings, you want your questions to come out naturally and in flow rather than having to think on the spot (this will break rapport). Therefore, take some time to plan these now and practice asking them so that they feel comfortable when you are in front of your prospect.

The more questions you have in your arsenal for each stage, the easier it is to draw on each of them during your sales meeting when things are moving at a hundred miles an hour.

## SCORE QUESTIONS

Symptom

.....................................................................................................................

.....................................................................................................................

.....................................................................................................................

Cause/Challenge

.....................................................................................................................

.....................................................................................................................

.....................................................................................................................

Outcome

.....................................................................................................................

.....................................................................................................................

.....................................................................................................................

Resource

.....................................................................................................................

.....................................................................................................................

.....................................................................................................................

Effect/Not Effect

.....................................................................................................................

.....................................................................................................................

.....................................................................................................................

**NEXT LEVEL PERSUASION**

# QUESTIONING MODEL - NEUROLOGICAL LEVELS

## IDENTITY
*Who?*

How do you see yourself in a particular situation? Identity may be easier to express as a metaphor. How would you describe yourself in a given role?

## VALUES
*Why?*

Values drive all decisions and hence behaviour. Understanding someone's values will give you an understanding of their motivation.

## BELIEFS
*Why?*

Our beliefs determine the actions we take in order to realise our values. Beliefs are typically generalisations of if/then statements.

## CAPABILITIES
*How?*

Your skill set and knowledge will influence your behaviour. Developing your skills will give you a wider range of behaviour choices.

## BEHAVIOR
*What?*

How do you spend your time? What are the main activities with which you fill your time? What are you saying and doing?

## ENVIRONMENT
*Where?*

Environment is everything outside of you, from the clothes you wear to your physical location and also the situation or context.

We have already explored the neurological levels model as a way of developing rapport with our prospects. However, it can also be used as a questioning model that allows you to ask questions that truly motivate your prospect into taking action. This is particularly useful when you are using a particularly emotional sales approach.

The neurological levels model allows us to identify the areas to make an impact that will facilitate lasting change. If we make a change higher in the model, this will impact all of the more superficial levels.

As a trainer, I have frequently been asked to impact the results that salespeople get by impacting their behaviour. The belief in training is that if you give people different skills and capabilities, their behaviour will change and this will impact their environment or results. However, I know so many salespeople that have the ability to sell, but they don't do what is required.

You have to ask yourself the question 'why'. Why do salespeople that have all the talent in the world not get the results that they are capable of? Why don't they do the activity that is required to earn the commissions they want and the company desires? Is there something holding them back? I have seen sales managers give motivational speeches on call days and salespeople respond with completely blank faces as if the message didn't even reach their ears. (If you are a sales manager, I guarantee you have sales people in your team that have a similar response!)

This applies to so many other areas of life as well. Why don't people lose weight when they know exactly what to do? Why don't people stop smoking when they know the exact impact of smoking on the body? If information was enough, everyone would be perfect already.

The truth is that giving new skills rarely impacts behaviour. Saying this will probably upset every sales trainer out there that teaches cold calling skills, or objection handling skills, and probably contradicts the vast majority of my book unless you understand one thing. Knowledge is only useful IF and only if that knowledge is put into practice.

If you think this book will make you the superstar salesperson that you have dreamed of becoming, it will not. There is no difference between a man that reads and does not learn and the man that cannot read. ACTION is the ultimate secret to success. Massive action, combined with learning through trial and error combined with coaching is the ultimate success formula. Without action, nothing matters.

So why don't knowledgeable, skilled sales people take action? The answer lies ABOVE their skills and capabilities, in the realms of beliefs, values and identity. This is also the area you need to ask questions if you are going to motivate your prospect to take the action you want them to take.

However, in order to ask these questions, you MUST have rapport! Don't think that you can ask the more probing questions without that mutual understanding of empathy that exists between two people in rapport. With no rapport, the same question appears rude and intrusive. With rapport, the question is transformed into a heartfelt enquiry into how best to serve your prospect. If you follow this process however, I guarantee that you will develop the rapport throughout the process that allows you to ask the deep probing questions.

> **Note** - If you are going to use this questioning model, you must be comfortable with silence. The questions you will be asking will probe into the mindset of your prospect and will not be easy to ask. There will be lots of pauses, and if you feel inclined to fill these by talking, you will lose the impact of this model. Become comfortable with putting your prospect on the spot and getting them to do the work rather than taking the edge off the situation.

## THE SECRET TO QUESTIONING WITH NEUROLOGICAL LEVELS

Want to know the secret behind using this model to motivate your prospect like never before? The way to do this is make a change at the IDENTITY level of the neurological levels model. By changing someone's identity of themselves, you will create a ripple effect that impacts all of the levels below. This will cause a change in values that impacts someone's motivation. You will change someone's beliefs which will determine the actions they take to fulfil their values. Assuming people have the skills required, this will lead to the change in behaviour that impacts the results they want to achieve. If you are ready to discover how to impact someone's identity, let's look at how to use the neurological levels as a questioning model.

BUT (isn't there always a but!) you have to ask ALL of the questions that lead to identity before you can ask that question. You also need to know how to use metaphors effectively to be successful with this questioning model.

## METAPHORS

A metaphor is a way of describing an entire concept by using an associated item. For example, the famous phrase by Shakespeare 'All the world's a stage' is a metaphor. When you consider this short sentence, a whole range of ideas spring to mind. We are always being observed. You have to act a certain way. In life, you have to pretend to be someone else.

To you and me this metaphor may mean something different to Shakespeare when he wrote it. However, as soon as we read it, we make the assumptions about life that are important to us. Metaphors are completely personal, and to ask someone to explain the finer details of their metaphor would require a very long, detailed conversation. However, if you continue to use the metaphor, you can bypass the requirement to understand everything completely.

In NLP, we call this idea 'Content Free'. Content free means that you do not need to know what is going on behind the metaphor, and instead you play with the words that your prospect is giving you.

The reason we use metaphors is because it is difficult to answer the question 'who are you?' in a way that encompasses the entirety of an individual. For example, your prospect may respond with their name, their job title or their relationship status, all of which only describe one particular element of their identity. By using a metaphor, we allow our prospect to describe themselves in a way that encompasses all aspects of their personality.

For example, if I was to ask you 'what kind of salesperson are you?', how would you respond? It might be difficult to answer this question. However, if I asked you to describe your current sales performance as a car, a sports team, a fashion designer, a band, a piece of food, a season or a world event, you will probably be able to give me an answer. If I asked you a follow up question of 'what kind of salesperson would you like to be?' then the chances are you will continue that same metaphor and give me an associated response.

This is how we are going to ask the identity level questions in the neurological levels model.

# NEUROLOGICAL LEVELS QUESTIONING MODEL

When you use the neurological levels model, your goal is to start at the bottom and work your way to the top in the current situation, move to the desired situation and then work your way down the model from identity down to the behaviours you want your prospect to take. Let's explore these questions below.

## CURRENT SITUATION

### Environment & Results
> Question - *What results are you currently getting?*
Here your prospect will tell you all of the ways their current activity is impacting their situation. As a sales person, get them to describe to you all of the effects that are unsatisfactory and get them to associate to the current situation which is not serving them.

### Behaviour
> Question - *How are you spending your time right now?*
Your goal is to highlight the ineffectiveness of your prospect's current activity. As soon as they tell you out loud that they are using their time ineffectively, you will find they instantly create the desire to change their behaviour. Avoid the urge to sell at this point and continue through the neurological levels model.

### Skills & Capabilities
> Question - *How did you learn how to do this?*
You will likely get a response about your prospect's history, how they ended up in their current role and how they came to take responsibility of the area you are questioning them on. You can potentially highlight some gaps in knowledge and skills that will be required to be successful in the areas they want to develop.

### Beliefs & Values

> *Question - What is driving your activity at this point?*

Expect responses that are outside of your prospect's control or influence, or modal operators of necessity. Take note of the limiting beliefs and values conflicts that exit within your prospect as you will want to use these later in your sales meeting.

### Identity

> *Question - How would you describe your current level of perform-ance? If you were to describe it as a XYZ, what would it be?*

*(XYZ is your chosen metaphor based on your prospect's interests.)*

This question will take time to answer. Avoid the need to fill the silence and instead wait patiently for your prospect's response. You will notice your prospect accessing all areas of the eye accessing cues before looking at you and responding. (If you are on the telephone, be patient!)

You now fully understand the challenges that your prospect is facing and have created an element of desire to change. DO NOT pitch at this point. Instead, trust in the process and come down through the neurological levels in the desired situation.

## DESIRED SITUATION

### Identity

> *Question - How do you describe the level you want to play at?*

Because you asked the questions back to back, the chances are your prospect will respond with an answer that is consistent with their metaphor. If their initial response was a takeaway meal, they will likely respond with a more extravagant meal. If they initially used a lower ...class car, the desired response will involve a more exclusive car. You do not need to know the full meaning behind the metaphor, but your prospect will. Use the idea of 'content free' to continue your questions and get your prospect to associate to this response.

### Beliefs & Values

> *Question - What is important to you now? What do you believe about your situation now?*

Notice the use of present, associative language. This will help create the emotional drive that will help close the sale. Because there will be multiple different possible responses, you may need to ask a follow up question to direct your prospect in the way you want them to think. This is the time for you to align their desired situation's values and beliefs with that of your product or service. If you are selling a time management tool, perhaps you ask the question 'how important to you is getting the most out of every day now?'. Because your prospect will be in a light trance, you can be a little more direct with your suggestive questions, although overdoing it will bring them out of trance immediately.

### Skills & Capabilities

> *Question - What do you need to be good at now? How did you develop that skill?*

Without the required skills, all the will and motivation in the world will be wasted. Ensure that your prospect knows HOW to close the gap between where they are and where they want to be. If you are selling training, this is a great time to explore the impact your product could potentially deliver. If you are a recruitment consultant, perhaps you ask about the skills and capabilities they have access to through the presence of other team members.

### Behaviour

> *Question - How do you spend your time differently now?*

True values are reflected in how people allocate their resources, especially time. By asking WHAT is done differently, you are checking that the identity and values shift has filtered down through to the behaviour level. By exploring this level, you are bringing the more subtle changes in mindset into reality which makes the whole shift tangible rather than purely hypothetical.

### Environment & Results

> *Question - What do you notice in your environment/results now?*

Change is all about seeing a different end result. This question should allow your prospect to see the true impact of the changes you are helping them to make. Make sure you ask follow up questions about the impact of your product on their results. For example, if you are selling print services, ask about how their clients respond to them when they see their promotional materials. If you are selling nutritional supplements, ask about how they look in the mirror or the compliments they get from friends or strangers.

The final step of the process is to bring your prospect back to their present state. This step helps to create an air of positive tension. You have just had your prospect associated to their goals and dreams, and made them believe that it is completely possible. Now, back in the present moment, they do not have any of those things, but they want them, and because you just showed them what was possible, they want to start on the journey of getting back to that desirable place. The feeling is akin to attaching an elastic band to them in their desired situation and then pulling them back to their current situation. Can you imagine what that tension would be like?

By asking this series of questions, you get a full understanding of your prospect's current situation as well as where they want to get to. You uncover the shortfalls in each of the neurological levels, and identify other angles to help your prospect succeed in make the change you are proposing to them. If you do this well, you will create a massive sense of motivation and urge to get started immediately. However, and possibly of greatest importance, you will have helped to create a lasting change, a change that permeates throughout that individual or organisation. This kind of holistic change impacts your prospect for the long-term, rather than just applying a sticky plaster as a temporary solution. This level of service will get your customers raving about you!

## SEEDING

Before we end this section on asking questions, I am often asked when you should start talking about your product or service, and I'll give you a clue... the bit on presenting is in the last section.

During a sales meeting, there are going to be various points when you are going to want to talk about your product. Don't! There will be beautiful moments where you have the ability to run through every function and button and widget that you can offer. Don't! Even if your prospect asks, don't give them the full pitch yet.

Why not?

If you went to a doctor and he wrote you a prescription before fully understanding your symptoms, how would you react? The same is true with sales. If you can't give an accurate prescription, you are speculating (guessing) that what you are telling them is exactly what they want. At best you will be able to give a generic presentation that gives an overview of your offering. You will not be able to do your product justice if you jump in too soon.

However, what you can do is drop in little bits of information in an indirect manner that gives your prospect a glimpse of what is to come, a bit like the previews that come before the movie at the cinema. Just like dropping seeds into the ground, you can then refer to these points throughout the meeting until you give your full presentation nearer the end.

Let me give you an example. You sell a product and offer a monthly payment whereas most of your competitors only accept payment up front. You ask a Cause question from the SCORE model - "So why haven't you done this before?" - and your prospect tells you that they have never been able to get the capital together to pay all in one go. The amateur salesperson would jump in at this point and pull out his payment plan summary and get straight into the pitch. However, there is a lot more information to gather first, so instead of pitching, seeding would involve saying:

*"Yes, those big payments can be a challenge. Wouldn't it be useful if someone could do the same but offer a payment plan."*

Notice how this is indirect and in no way talking about your product or service. What reaction do you think the following response would get.

*"Yes, all those other companies are unreasonable but we offer a payment plan which is great isn't it!"*

Even if you aren't getting into your full pitch, talking about yourself at this early stage in the meeting makes you seem like you are interested in yourself and your product more than your prospect. If your prospect feels as though you are trying to line up a list of advantages to convince them towards the end, do you think this will encourage them to be open during your conversation? If your prospect isn't giving you the whole picture, you will struggle to win the deal.

So, wait until the end before you even mention your company, product or service. When the opportunity arises to talk about what you can offer, resist and instead drop in an idea that relates to what you can offer in a way that is indirect but would ultimately be a benefit to your prospect.

Poor educators teach facts. Great educators teach the same facts but help the student develop the understanding of the facts by asking the right questions. Great salespeople show just enough information, but rather than 'telling' what to do, ask great questions that allow the prospect to come to the appropriate conclusion in their own mind. Of course, these great salespeople knew exactly what the answer to the question was before they asked it, but they realised the value in allowing their prospect to come to that realisation themselves rather than it being thrust upon them. Your job is to know what questions to ask and when to bring your customer round to your way of thinking.

**Here are some of the main points to take away from this chapter.**

- Never ask a question you do not know the answer to. Unless you are genuinely uncovering information, you should always know what your prospect is going to say. Then, you work backwards and develop the perfect question to elicit that response.

- Your language directs the imagination of your prospect throughout the sales meeting. By using the hypnotic language patterns particularly, you can create powerful imagery that will not just aid understanding of your solution, but also begin to create both attachment and desire.

- The questions you ask will follow the stepping stones of the path you set, but you must always be prepared to go off-piste. Never be so regimented in your sales approach that you miss vital information because it isn't on the script. Just remember to mark where you went off track so you can get back.

- Ultimately, your questions need to leave your prospect with a gap from where they are currently to where they want to be. That gap needs to be big and scary and they need to know the one and only way to close that gap successfully. I wonder what that solution might be!

# CHAPTER 8
# MOTIVATING

| OPENING | CONNECTING | EDUCATING | MOTIVATING | COMMITTING |
|---------|------------|-----------|------------|------------|

| PREPARING |
|-----------|

| PURPOSE |
|---------|

*"Arouse in the other person an eager want. He who can do this has the whole world with him. He who cannot walks a lonely way."*

**- Dale Carnegie**

*"If you want to build a ship, don't drum up people together to collect wood and don't assign them tasks and work, but rather teach them to long for the endless immensity of the sea."*

**- Antoine de Saint-Exupéry**

You know when you look at the sun and then close your eyes and you can still see the shape of the sun? That's probably similar to how your eyes feel about seeing this definition of sales:

*Sales is getting someone to do something*

*that you want them to do,*

*whether they realize they want to do it yet or not.*

One of the key elements in this definition is 'getting someone to do something', take some form of action as a result of the interaction. If you are effectively educating your prospect throughout the sales process, then they will understand the decision and the action that they need to take. However, if they are not motivated to make that choice, you will probably hear them say "I'll think about it".

You probably already know that all purchase decisions are made emotionally and then justified logically. Therefore, if the educating process of Next Level Persuasion is impacting your client in a logical way then the motivating stage is interested in the emotional drivers to the decision.

One of the biggest time wasting elements of a salesperson's role is following up those people that said 'maybe'. 'Maybe' can come in lots of different disguises such as 'I need to discuss this with my partner', 'can you send me over some more information' or 'give me a couple of weeks and I'll have an answer for you', but effectively, they all mean the same thing - your prospect is thinking logically, not emotionally. You schedule callback after callback and they keep palming you off another week or two with the same old excuses but you keep telling yourself they are going to come in eventually.

If you have had this experience then the chances are that you made a great logical argument for buying your product or service, but just didn't connect with their emotional drivers.

Before you think this is getting fluffy and doesn't apply to business-to-business situations, think again. In 1980s during the recession, the computer company IBM ran an advertising campaign with the slogan "No One Ever Got Fired for Buying IBM". This was aimed at people in companies purchasing IT equipment which you would imagine would be one of the most logical decisions possible. However, IBM knew that even though these decisions needed to be justified logically, the actual purchase would be made based emotionally, and during the depression, the key worry everyone had was job security. If you could show how buying your product would ensure job security people would most certainly be interested.

Naturally, the motivating factors and values that apply in a business-to-business sales environment will be different to someone selling directly to consumers, but in reality, every product or service that exists targets different values or combinations of values. It isn't just purchasing decisions that are made emotionally either. In fact, every decision we make throughout the day can be tied to one of our personal drivers, or values, and once you understand which values apply to a particular individual, you can almost predict their behaviour in any given context.

Marketing has understood the power of values for a long time and has exploited this to boost brand appeal and break into new markets. However, marketing has an advantage over sales... marketing doesn't have to make any sense!

Think about a marketing campaign for a soft drink. It wants to target young people and decides that this target market wants to be cool, experience adventure and break all the rules. So what does the marketing agency do? They create an advert with snowboarding, parachuting, and white-water rafting and then show these same people enjoying their soft drink in exotic locations.

In the viewer's mind, the following association occurs. The young person associates to the people in the advert having fun and experiencing excitement and starts getting into that state themselves (when we watch television we are in a light trance anyway so are highly suggestible). At the same time as being in this emotional state, they see the soft drink product. If this connection or neuro-association occurs often enough or with enough emotional intensity, the two will become linked in the mind of the viewer. Now, whenever you think about that soft drink, you associate the feelings of being cool, adventure and breaking the rules that all the people in the advert experienced.

Although he probably had no idea of it's marketing appeal at the time, Ivan Pavlov discovered this form of classical conditioning when experimenting with the salivation response of dogs whilst ringing bells. Of course, it doesn't stop at soft drinks. Malboro invented the Malboro Man and Malboro Country to make the brand more masculine and attract more male customers at a time when it was considered a feminine cigarette. Cadbury's advertised their Flake bar with a woman lying in an overflowing bath more focussed on the chocolate than the inevitable clean up that was to follow. And what do meerkats have to do with insurance anyway?

All marketers need to do is get you into the emotional state they want you in and then show you their product... simples!

So, sales certainly needs to use emotion and understand motivation and values, but rather than doing it on a mass scale, salespeople need to understand the values of the individual in front of them.

Without a doubt one of the best books on understanding innate human psychology for persuasion is the book Influence: The Psychology Of Persuasion by Robert Cialdini and I cannot recommend this book highly enough to salespeople (I mentioned this in the personal development list in the Preparing section too). In this book, Cialdini describes the results of his psychological experiments into persuasion and summarises the key ways that you can influence a person's behaviour.

**Scarcity** - limiting the availability of a product.

**Reciprocity** - give someone something so they feel as though they owe you.

**Likeable** - we are more likely to do something for someone we like.

**Authority** - we tend to do something if told by someone in authority.

**Commitment & Consistency** - if I said I am that way, I will act accordingly.

**Social Proof** - if everyone else is doing it, why aren't you?

You can use each of these factors to motivate someone to take action, and as much as I would love to go into this subject in more detail, I wouldn't want you to not read Influence, so make sure to get yourself a copy of that book. There are a few great linguistic patterns and constructs in that book which I am sure you will also enjoy.

However, these are innate psychological patterns that we can manipulate in order to get people to take action without question. As we have already discussed, if we do this without integrity, we are going against the whole concept of Next Level Persuasion and will perpetuate the bad image of salespeople. Instead, when you consider these techniques, think about how you can use them within the concepts of Next Level Persuasion, and I will include a few examples as we go through.

The focus of this section on Motivating is going to focus on understanding the driving factors, or values, of our prospects and customers. Once we understand why people do what they do and what influences the decisions they make in a given context, we can effectively position ourselves and our product in a way that matches exactly what they want.

## UNDERSTANDING VALUES

Values: a collection of guiding, usually positive principles; what one deems to be correct and desirable in life, especially regarding personal conduct.

Values are the emotions that drive all human behaviour. Everything we do in life results from our beliefs that a particular action will help us to achieve that particular feeling.

Think about it. Why are you reading this book? Is it because your education is important to you? Is it because you want to earn more commission and you believe that learning these skills will improve your earning potential? Whatever the reason, it will be tapping into one of your life's values. Anything you do on a regular basis can be tied to one or more of your values.

A value can be identified if your prospect uses a single word or short phrase. For example, adventure is a value that many people hold, as is peace of mind.

Understanding your prospect's values is critical to your success in selling effectively. Once you truly understand what values are and how they shape decisions, you will actually be able to predict the choices prospects make in any given context.

In this section, you will learn to become a master at understanding and working with values. In order to do this, you need to learn three steps:

1. Values Elicitation
2. Values Hierarchy
3. Values Alignment

## VALUES ELICITATION

When you first elicit someone's values, your goal is to uncover all of the things that motivate and drive that particular individual. To do that, simply ask the following question:

*What is important to you about XYZ?*

This simple question will help you to identify the values that a person has around whichever context you decide. For example, if you want to find out your prospect's life values, you ask 'what is important to you in life?'. If you are selling to a company, perhaps you modify the question slightly to 'what is important to the business?'.

> **Note** - If you are going to delve into a conversation with your prospect about their values, it is important to have a suitable level of rapport. Asking questions about desires and fears requires an element of trust between the salesperson and the prospect. Also, as these questions will require a certain amount of thinking time to properly formulate an answer, you will need to be comfortable with a certain amount of silence following your question.

Below is a list of 100 of the most common values that you will encounter.

---

  **NEXT LEVEL PERSUASION**

| | | | |
|---|---|---|---|
| Abundance | Energy | Joy | Prosperity |
| Achievement | Entertainment | Knowledge | Punctuality |
| Adventure | Environmentalism | Leadership | Recognition |
| Affection | Excellence | Longevity | Recreation |
| Ambition | Extroversion | Love | Reflection |
| Audacity | Faith | Loyalty | Respect |
| Balance | Family | Making a difference | Responsibility |
| Being the best | Fidelity | Meaning | Security |
| Celebrity | Financial | Mindfulness | Sensuality |
| Certainty | Fitness | Modesty | Service |
| Challenge | Focus | Motivation | Significance |
| Charity | Freedom | Nature | Sincerity |
| Community | Friendship | Noncomformity | Spirituality |
| Competition | Fun | Open-mindedness | Spontaneity |
| Conformity | Gratitude | Optimism | Strength |
| Connection | Growth | Organization | Success |
| Contribution | Happiness | Peace | Teaching |
| Control | Health | Perfection | Teamwork |
| Creativity | Honesty | Philanthropy | Thankfulness |
| Determination | Independence | Playfulness | Uniqueness |
| Discipline | Individuality | Popularity | Variety |
| Diversity | Inspiration | Power | Vitality |
| Drive | Integrity | Pragmatism | Volunteering |
| Economy | Intelligence | Pride | Wealth |
| Education | Intimacy | Privacy | Wisdom |

*(For a list of even more values, as well as other awesome ideas, check out http://www.stevepavlina.com/articles/list-of-values.htm)*

When exploring values in a coaching or therapy situation, you might look to uncover around 10 values for any area you are questioning. For example, if you are trying to uncover somebody's life values (what is important to you in life?), the chances are that there will be a number of driving factors that motivate them.

Try it for yourself below. What are your life values? Write down any words that come to mind, whether you think they are a value or not. As you get more experienced, you will begin to recognise values in language whatever the context.

## WHAT IS IMPORTANT TO ME ABOUT LIFE?

.........................................................................................................................................................

.........................................................................................................................................................

.........................................................................................................................................................

.........................................................................................................................................................

.........................................................................................................................................................

.........................................................................................................................................................

.........................................................................................................................................................

.........................................................................................................................................................

How did you get on? What did you discover both about yourself as well as about the process? Did you manage to write down ten values?

The chances are that on your list of values you have some words that seem to contradict each other. For example, did you have Security as one of your values, but also Adventure? Did you have Power as one of your values, but also Teamwork?

This is known as a Values Conflict. We regularly have values that seem to pull us in opposite directions. When we look at our values hierarchy in the next section, we will learn more about how the rank order of our values impacts how we live our lives. However, for right now, just understand that sometimes we have motivation that pulls us toward both polar opposites.

The other aspect to consider when understanding values is the rules we place on these values in order to meet them. These criteria will determine whether this value acts as Toward or Away From motivation for you. All values can act from either perspective and will move you ultimately in the same direction. However, the level of motivation varies for each.

Toward Motivation is like dangling a carrot in front of you. There is something to strive for, a goal or a desired outcome that is important to the individual. With toward motivation, we can set a goal, achieve it and then set a further goal without losing our drive and passion.

Away From Motivation works much like a thermostat. If your climate gets too hot or too cold, the thermostat kicks in to initiate the appropriate cooling or heating activity. Once back in the accepted range, the thermostat no longer needs to be working. Away from motivation can provide a huge amount of immediate motivation, but this fades as we get further away from our internal set point.

Let's look at Health for example.

Some people have health as a toward value. The way health motivates them is to achieve a particular body shape, level of fitness or other measure of physical fitness. For these people they are constantly motivated to exercise, eat healthily and make decisions that will support this lifestyle. This is reflected in their everyday behaviour and activity. They may challenge themselves a little further each year, especially if they reach major objectives.

On the other hand, some people have health as an away from value. They realise health is important, but the way these people view it is that they don't want to be too unhealthy, too overweight or too out of shape. When they realise they are getting close to their set point of unacceptability, they are spurred into action. Suddenly they go to the gym twice a day for a week, eat healthily every day, cut out chocolate and walk everywhere. At the end of a week, they are far enough away from their set point to be able to relax and then go back to their normal routine. Of course, this gradually leads back to the set point and another week of intense activity. I'm sure you know people like this.

All values have the potential to motivate in either a toward or away from manner. People motivated by success might want to be the best, or not be a failure. People with the value of love may want to have an incredible relationship, or may not want to feel lonely. Those who have adventure on

---

their values list may want to have experiences that excite them, or may not want to be bored.

## VALUES ELICITATION IN SALES

When in a sales situation, asking about life values may seem a little strange. Instead, ask for the values around the purchase. Rather than pushing for 10 values, identify the top two or three that are important to your prospect. Questions might include:

- What is driving this purchase right now?
- Why have you decided to consider this option?
- What are the business goals for this project?

If you know the individual you are dealing with and have an understanding about their lifestyle, you may get an insight into this person's personal life values. However, be careful with the assumption that the values for the purchase are the same. Values are contextual. People may be very security focussed at home, but at work are a lot more adventurous.

Business values may sound a little different to personal values, but still act in the same way. For example, business growth could either be to take control of the market place or to avoid getting swallowed up by the competition. When dealing with a business sales situation, you will want to understand both the business values and your prospect's individual vales as well.

**Some common business goals are:**

| | |
|---|---|
| Communication | Continuous Improvement |
| Customer Service | Developing People |
| Efficiency | Innovation |
| Integrity | Responsiveness |
| Social Enterprise | Timeliness |

## VALUES HIERARCHY

Now you know which values your prospect or business deems important, you need to know the order of importance. Understanding this will make the difference between someone liking what you tell them and someone crying out for more of what you have to offer.

Let's say that on your list of values you have both security and adventure. (Most people have both of these in some format in their list of values.) The value that is higher in your hierarchy will tend to be more dominant in your decision making. So let me ask you a question.

*'Would you be interested in doing a bungee jump?'*

If you answered 'yes' then the chances are your adventure value is more important to you than security. If you answered 'no freaking way!' and had a minor panic attack, there is a very good chance that security is very close to the top of your hierarchy.

By understanding somebody's value hierarchy, you can predict the decisions they are likely to make in any given context. Can you see how this might be useful in sales?

**How do you find out a person's hierarchy?**

There are three main ways to uncover an individual's values hierarchy:

- Ask them

- Look at how they allocate their resources

- A or B Method

## ASK THEM

If you have elicited someone's values, you can then ask them to rank them in order of importance. Whilst this seems to be the simplest way, it is likely to be the least accurate of the three methods.

For example, you have discovered that your prospect has both social responsibility and also leisure and recreation time on their values list. If you ask them which is more important to them, they may feel the need to give you a more socially acceptable answer. Not many people would admit to valuing free time and relaxation over serving the needs of their community, but that might be exactly how this person acts. However, because they do not want to appear this way, they may switch their perception of the order of their values to put themselves in a better light.

If you are going to use this method, always check using the following method, which is to look at how they use their resources.

## LOOK AT HOW THEY ALLOCATE THEIR RESOURCES

If you are dealing with a business that says innovation is top of their values list, how many people are in their research and development department. If you are dealing with an individual that says they value self-control, but who overeats, bites their nails or chain-smokes, you may have incongruence.

How a person allocates their resources is the true test of their values. Resources can be words such as money, time, energy, focus, attention, staff, budget or manpower.

Two people have health and fitness as a value as well as fashion and personal image. Person A has health and fitness ahead of fashion and personal image whereas Person B is flipped the other way. They both need to buy a pair of shoes and a pair of trainers. Who do you think spends more on shoes than trainers and who spends more trainers than shoes?

Although this is a very basic example, can you see how observing a person's actions and how they allocate their resources can give you an insight into their true values and the associated hierarchy?

## A OR B METHOD

In this final method, you are still asking your prospect's opinion as in the first method. This time, instead of ranking the whole list in one go, you are looking for them to tell you which value out of two is more important. This should give you a more accurate response if you do one of two things:

- Instinctive response

- Polarise responses

Let's use family and career success as two potential values. Many people have both of these values somewhere in their hierarchy and often they come into conflict with resource allocation. By using the A or B method, you should quickly be able to identify which is more important that the other.

*Which is more important to you, Value A or Value B?*

With the instinctive response, simply ask for the first answer that springs to mind. If people think too long, they rationalise and have a tendency to give a more socially acceptable response. By eliminating thinking time, you are encouraging the person to respond from their unconscious, which will be closer to the truth.

When you polarise the responses, highlighting the extremes of each potential response. This is useful if your prospect is unsure, hesitant or giving an incongruent answer. In this case, you might ask a follow up question such as:

*Would you rather have great career success but do it alone, or would you prefer to have an incredibly rich relationship but work in a mediocre job?*

By making the extremes more obvious, you will likely find that your prospect associates with one of the outcomes more than the other. The fact is that your prospect would like somewhere in between, but the extreme to which they lean will let you know which value is higher in the hierarchy.

Once you have gone through each of the values and assessed its relevant merits against the others, you will have an ordered list of values which we call a values hierarchy. Use the space below to write your values in the order they appear in your hierarchy.

**MY VALUES HIERARCHY**

_____

_____

_____

_____

_____

_____

_____

Finally, once you know which values are most important to your prospect or the company, you need to align yourself and your product or service to that hierarchy.

# VALUES ALIGNMENT

Imagine you had met a prospect with the following values hierarchy:

1. Success
2. Competition
3. Integrity
4. Security
5. Socialisation

For the purposes of this example, you are trying to sell this person a job. Which job description do you think they would prefer?

**Job Description A**

Long standing fun company filled with numerous like-minded people that love working together. Many of our employees have been working with the company for over 10 years, and we put that down to our commitment to making sure that all employees are taken care of and put into roles that best suit their skillset. Every year, we encourage our employees to give back to the community by arranging events which raise money for our chosen charities and causes.

**Job Description B**

If you want to be the best, we want you. Driven company looking for driven individuals who know what it takes to play on the winning team. We promise the very best training and development, but we are looking for people with the drive and determination it takes to make it happen. We are a social enterprise and regularly give back to the local community, and have a compulsory week each year where our employees take part in community work to help those less fortunate. The person who makes the biggest difference is given a sizeable donation to the charity of their choice, and then it is right back to work.

Which job do you think your prospect would prefer? I imagine that the prospect would be far more excited by job description B.

However, is it possible that those two descriptions were talking about the same opportunity? Of course it is. For every product and service in the marketplace, there are hundreds of different ways to describe the item and its features and benefits that tie in with someone's values.

Values alignment is the process of matching you, your business or your product's features with the values of your prospect. This means you need to understand how each of the elements of what you are selling can be positioned in a way that connects with a particular value.

For example, you work for a small, local printing company and are pitching to a restaurant that wants to get new menus printed each month. How would you position yourself in a way that aligns with this business? Perhaps you could use the small size of your business as an indicator of how

---

flexible and responsive you are which would facilitate the monthly updates. Perhaps being local will mean you can do more face-to-face design consultations which will allow the client to create menus that truly reflect the quality of the restaurant.

There are so many ways to align yourself, your company or your product with another person's values. Lets see how you get on with the activity below. For each, write out a way that you can align with this particular value:

Success

_____

_____

_____

Family

_____

_____

_____

Environmental

_____

_____

_____

Social Responsibility

_____

_____

_____

Teamwork

_____

_____

_____

Once you have mastered the ability to elicit values, discover the hierarchy and then align yourself, you will be able to motivate any prospect to buy what you want them to buy. As long as what you are offering is matched closely enough to their values, they will want what you have to offer them.

By understanding the process of Motivating, you are able to create a desire within your prospect for the very product or service you have to offer. Without motivation and interest, it is going to be difficult to sell anything. However, by motivating, you stop being a salesperson and position yourself as the person that can help your prospect buy their perfect solution. They want it. They know they need it. And they know they can only get it from you. Once you get your prospects to a point where they are asking to buy from you, that is when you know you have become a master of motivation.

**Here are some of the main points to take away from this chapter.**

- All purchases are made emotionally and justified with logic. If you do not get into the real motivation behind this potential purchase, you will miss what is driving the conversation, and unless they come to you pre-motivated (dream client) they will probably hear 'I need to think about it'.

- Human behaviour is driven by our values, and these same values determine the decisions we make in any given context. By understanding your prospect's values, you know the boxes you and your product need to tick in order to really raise the excitement about your offering.

- Positive motivation will create interest but negative motivation can create real urgency. Don't just talk about how great your solution will be, make sure your prospect is crystal clear on exactly what will happen if they leave without buying what you have to offer.

- As values drive all behaviour, you don't just have to rely on your prospect's words to understand them. How does your client spend their free time? Why do you think that might be? Look beyond the sales meeting to get valuable contextual information about your prospect's values hierarchy.

# CHAPTER 9
# COMMITTING

| OPENING | CONNECTING | EDUCATING | MOTIVATING | COMMITTING |
|---------|-----------|-----------|------------|------------|
| PREPARING | | | | |
| PURPOSE | | | | |

*"You must never try to make all the money that's in a deal. Let the other fellow make some money too, because if you have a reputation for always making all the money, you won't have many deals."*

**- J. Paul Getty**

*"The way you position yourself at the beginning of a relationship has profound impact on where you end up."*

**- Ron Karr**

Before you start this section, take a deep breath.

If you have got this far into the sales process, you should have a great connection with a prospect who has been educated to know what he or she needs and who is motivated to make the decision. If you have effectively followed each of the steps of Next Level Persuasion, your prospect will be excited to hear about your product or service and be keen to get started on the next steps as soon as possible.

So why is there so much apprehension about the closing stage of a sales meeting?

The answer is that, in the past, the focus of the sales process has been on the close and the clever linguistic patterns that can get prospects to agree to buy even when they aren't really interested. Those salespeople only ever created superficial rapport and certainly didn't understand the reasons behind the purchase. All they were interested in was pitching and closing, pitching and closing. If you don't have the rapport and the connection with your prospect then yes, you better be outstanding at closing because that is all you have.

In the committing stage of the sale, this is where you highlight the exact actions you want your client to take by presenting your solution which you will have tailored to meet their needs exactly. Then, you need to artfully deal with any objections that arise in a way that maintains both the rapport you have built as well as the momentum of the sales process. Finally, once your prospect agrees with everything you have laid out in front of them, you have to ask them that final closing question and get them to commit to the deal and sign the cheque. (Does anyone still use cheques? Signing a contract is nice but there is something even more satisfying about watching someone sign a cheque with your name on it!)

Maintaining your state throughout this whole section is vital as when you get closer to your goal, your body and mind become more 'excited'. For some, this excitement makes them speak faster, or get sweaty palms. For others, the adrenalin can distract them and make them forget about the basics. This is what the deep breath was for, to help you slow back down and compose yourself before finishing the sales meeting in style and with a positive outcome. Once you are on the other side of the successful sale and out of eyeline and earshot of your new customer, then you can let it all go and celebrate like crazy. However, until that point, keep it together.

So, by now, your questions should have uncovered the challenges your prospect faces, their goals and ambitions and why they want to make this change in their circumstances. But up until this point, you haven't really talked at all about your product or service. Before I tell you why, I want you to read the below phrase and memorise it:

*There is nothing worse than premature... pitching!*

Believe me, there will have been times during the meeting where you will have wanted to tell your prospect all about what you do and all the bells and whistles your product can offer. However, I want you to resist and not say anything about your solution until you get to this point.

Have you ever watched the film The Sixth Sense? << SPOILER ALERT>> In this movie, Bruce Willis plays a psychologist who is helping a young boy who can see dead people, ghosts walking around acting just like people because they don't know they are dead. As they go through the movie, there are little twists and turns which the viewer does not understand until right at the end of the movie when it turns out that Bruce Willis is also a ghost! The movie then flashes back to those points and shows them from a different perspective that allow you to make sense of the entire movie. It is that great twist at the end of the movie which keeps you enthralled throughout and that is exactly how you want your prospect to be during your sales meeting.

Can you imagine how different the movie would have been if you had found out the big twist right from the start? The engagement would be massively reduced and the positive tension would have dissipated.

You want your prospects to have a level of excitement that keeps them engaged until you know you are ready to present them with their ideal solution. In fact, you almost want your prospect to get to this point of the sales meeting and be asking you what it is you are going to offer them. Can you imagine a prospect begging to hear about your product? That is a very different experience than what happens for most salespeople who don't understand Next Level Persuasion.

So having built up enough tension throughout, you are now ready to present your solution to your prospect, but how do you do this? Let's look at exactly how we put together our product pitch for our soon-to-be client.


## PRESENTING YOUR SOLUTION

People buy for emotional reasons and then justify it with logic.

What I have noticed with a lot of sales people is that they tend to choose either one approach or the other, often depending on the product or service being sold. However, to be effective, both emotional and logical perspectives must be utilised.

Take, for example, a salesperson selling a financial product. These are often sold emotionally: fear of loss for insurance or massive upside for exotic investments. However, if only the dream is sold, then although the prospect may purchase, they will soon be asked by someone what they have actually bought. If the prospect is not able to describe the product in detail, beyond merely the dream concept, then they will likely experience buyers remorse. The next day, you get a call and you have to refund the deal.

Contrast that with the advertising product that may give you slightly better returns than other products. All of the numbers add up, and there is definitely a small benefit to be had. It would seem that this is a simple decision to make, but instead the salesperson is greeted with the worst possible response - 'I'll think about it!' This response is when the prospect is not motivated enough to take action.

You absolutely need to include elements of both emotional selling as well as logical justification when selling any product.

This is true even when selling in a business-to-business environment. However, you may find it described differently. In B2B environments, people buy for their personal interest, but justify it on the basis of business requirements.

## FBI STATEMENTS

An FBI statement is not something you need to give if you commit a felony in the United States. Instead, it is the way you should structure each element of your final presentation.

All too often, presentations are given solely about the details or features of a product, and this is never the way to sell. Let me give you an example of how this can go horribly wrong.

I needed to buy a vacuum cleaner one particular day after a rather unsuccessful day of DIY at home. I had managed to create a small pile of dust and rubble and my existing vacuum just didn't want to play. I headed down to the nearest appliance store and began inspecting the vacuum cleaners on offer. As this was in the days before the iPhone and I had no idea of what consisted of a good vacuum, I decided to ask one of the store's employees for some assistance.

"Is this a good vacuum?" I asked the shop assistant. I could tell instantly that I had chosen the wrong person entirely as there was a slightly blank look on his face. In all credit to him though, he did attempt to answer, but unfortunately for me, all he did was read the card that was placed in front of the vacuum.

"It has 1200 RPM sir!" he replied with an implied sense of excitement. "4.5 litres of storage and 4500 watts of power!". (I am making these numbers up as I am still none the wiser about vacuums!). I asked him about the vacuum cleaner next to it and got the same reading-from-the-card response.

I could see for myself what the features were. I could see how many RPM and how many watts and how long the cable was but I didn't know what any of that stuff meant! Would it be enough to clear up my mess and any subsequent mess that resulted from other DIY projects? I thanked the shop assistant for his time but felt that the whole interaction had been a waste of time.

(On a bit of a rant, estate agents can also be pretty terrible at this. If you have ever had an estate agent show you around a property and they tell you what each room is, you will know what I mean. "This is the kitchen". "Oh really Sherlock, I am so glad you are here with your useful insights! I was starting to wonder why someone had stuck an oven in the middle of the bathroom, but now everything is clear!" Estate agents, please promise me you will never do this again. Rant over!)

So if just talking about features is not the correct way to sell something, then what is the answer?

Old school sales training talked about Features, Advantages and Benefits, but let me ask you a question: What is the difference between an Advantage and a Benefit? I could never figure this out. The only way it made sense to me was if you were comparing yourself to some other product, in which case your sales pitch became a my-product-is-better-than-their-product approach. This may have been fine when there were only a couple of options, but today, our customers have so many different options to choose from, and one of those options is to not do anything. This means you have to be able to give a stand-alone pitch which is non comparative. How do you do that?

## FBI - FEATURE. BENEFIT. IMPACT.

FBI statements use features, benefits and impacts to give all the reasons somebody should choose your product or service. We are still going to use the features that our vacuum salesperson was so eloquent in reading, but we are also going to talk about what that means to the customer, both in a generic sense as well as a specific sense. We are also going to tie in the concepts of emotional and logical selling to ensure we cover both reasons that people buy.

Let's look at what each of these elements are before we compile our own FBI statements.

### Features

Features are the specific details or component parts of your product or service. If you sell photocopiers, then perhaps your photocopier has a maximum print rate of 30 sheets per minute or has wireless printing capabilities. If you run a cleaning company, perhaps you offer a 24 hour, round the clock service, or all of your staff are trained in how to use the chemical products you work with. These details are what you have to sell, and there will likely be hundreds, if not thousands of these for each aspect of your business.

Your challenge is not to try and sell every feature of your business, rather sell the ones that your prospect wants to buy. Too often, sales people get into the habit of listing every single feature that their product has, the result being that the useful parts that the prospect wanted get drowned out in the noise of all the others. This is why your questioning and listening are so important BEFORE you get to the pitch. How can you pitch something effectively when you don't really know what they want?

*Your pitch needs to be PRESCRIPTIVE,*
*not SPECULATIVE!*

When you go to the doctor, you are hoping for a prescription, a specific suggestion for medicine that will cure the particular ailment from which you are suffering. You don't expect to go to the doctor and have this conversation:

Doctor:
*"What can I do for you?"*

Patient:
*"I'm not feeling very well."*

Doctor:
*"Well what I suggest is taking some paracetamol and ibuprofen*
*for the pain, let's give you some antihistamines in case you have*
*an allergic    reaction, throw in a few antibiotics in case you have*
*an infection, better give you a few jabs and inoculations in case*
*you have a nasty disease, some malaria tablets won't hurt*
*either... anything else?"*

You need to decide on the key aspects of your product and then make these the focus of your presentation. Prescribe a solution rather than speculating what the prospect needs. If you find your presentations are not hitting the spot, then perhaps you need to look at your questioning and listening skills from the exploration part of the sale.

## Benefit

Once you have identified a particular feature, you need to tie it to a benefit. A benefit is what that particular feature will give you as a result. If you have ever been on a sales training course, you will no doubt have heard of the acronym WIIFM meaning 'What's In It For Me?'. The benefit is what is in it for your prospect.

Let's go back to the photocopier salesperson and look at the wireless printing feature. What are the benefits of this to the prospect? Well, the fact is that there are a number of potential benefits that this feature could link to, and this will be the same for your product and features too. For example, wireless printing could allow anyone to come into the office and print documents out. It could mean that you would not need a complete cabling restructure that often accompanies new hardware installation. It could mean that people outside of the office could print documents either on the road or from home.

The challenge again with your benefits is not listing them all, but instead tying them to the associated problems or challenges that you are helping to solve with your product. If you have listened to your prospect, and he complained about the last time they got a new printer they had to upgrade the cabling then you know which benefit you would tie into. If the prospect talks about the rapid growth of the team, then tie into how this feature allows for new users without any problems.

For the features of your product or service, you will also have a number of associated benefits. Your first job is to start thinking about all of the ways you can take a feature and give the prospect the WIIFM.

You will find that the benefits you give are both short term and generic. For example, having a printer that allows for the growth of the team is not specific to this particular prospect. You could probably use this same combination with a number of other prospects and have something that works. Also, the growth of the team is a here and now challenge, so this benefit is going to apply immediately.

Remember, people often want things to happen now. As a species, we are pretty impatient, which is not a bad thing in itself as it drives innovation such as faster transport links and technology. However, by showing your prospect that there will be an immediate benefit, you increase your chances of selling.

Remember we talked about the fact that people are driven by 3 factors for action? These were Massive, Immediate and Pain and during your presentation, you need t o remember these. If you can show the immediate benefits of your product, you will dramatically increase the desire for your prospect to take action now.

## Impact

The impact is what the feature and benefit mean directly to your prospect, rather than just the generic benefits that everyone gets. Of course, the logical thing would be to go for something that has an immediate benefit and makes sense, but since when did anyone by for the logical reason? We need to bring some emotion into the pitch.

Impact statements tie into the values of your prospect, so you can see now why it is important to ask these questions during the sales process. Remember, values are the motivating force behind action, and will literally drive the person to do the things that they believe will allow them to realise their values.

Remember, action is a salesperson's best friend. Maybe doesn't help anybody!

If you understand the values of your prospect and what is important to them about this potential purchase, then you can align their values with those of your product to create a very powerful presentation.

Let's go back to our photocopier salesperson. He is talking about wireless printing options that allow new people to join the printing network with ease. During the conversation, you discover that two of the driving forces or values of your prospect are that they really want to grow the business to be able to leave it for their family, but also that they are working so many hours that the amount of time they currently spend at home is being affected. Family, therefore, is one this person's key values.

The impact aspect of this feature needs to tie back to the values. Instead of being generic and immediate, we want to amplify these and make them personal. This covers the massive factor for action, but to do this, we may need to extrapolate the time aspect, which removes the immediacy. However, we have already covered this in our benefit statement.

The impact statement then should link back to how the wireless printing facility will allow people to join the network with ease, which means the prospect is free to grow the business without having to worry about constantly making changes to the infrastructure. This should also in turn free up more time, which could even be spent with the family as they are growing up.

In truth, your product can tie into ANY of the values that your prospect may have. If you think about the vast number of benefits that each feature may have, you can easily find a way to tie these back to the core values that you will uncover with your prospects. The number of values that will drive purchases for your particular product or service are limited, so get good at bringing the conversation and your pitch back to these values and really making the emotional side of the purchase obvious.

## VALUES ALIGNMENT

If you can show how the values of your product or service inherently tie into the values of your prospect or their business, then you have a very strong connection that will assist you in closing the sale. To do this, make sure you are clear on what YOUR values are, either for you, your product or your company. As you are going through your questioning and exploring process and you uncover your prospect's values, seed ideas that you or your product ties into these, but avoid jumping into a full pitch. Continuing with the photocopier example, when you find out that family is important, perhaps you can relay a testimonial from a client that was able to spend less time working as a result of the work you did together. Values alignment, as with any sales technique, needs to be artfully done. Any obvious alignment techniques will have the opposite effect on your prospect and will come across as slick and manipulative.

Does this work for Business to Business?

The simple answer is yes, it does work, but there are certain caveats that you need to be aware of.

Firstly, business decisions are rarely made on the spur of the moment. This means that the emotional side of selling will wear off before the final decision is made. If you rely too heavily on emotional selling, you may find that you get a great reaction during your presentation but that the deal goes to someone else.

Secondly, you may find that the final decision is not made by just one person. If this is the case, how do you choose whose values to align to? In this situation, there are a couple of options. Firstly, identify core values that each decision maker and influencer have in common. Use these as your core value and build your presentation around this. Alternatively, look at the company's mission statement. This will usually give a clear indication as to the corporate vision and values and if you align to this, you should get the buy in from all of the stakeholders. This works particularly with larger organisations that tend to spend time promoting their company's core values.

## FUTURE PACING

In NLP, future pacing allows you to check the efficacy of your intervention by investigating future events in which the previous behavioural challenge would have arisen. Have you as a coach been successful and have your suggestions embedded themselves effectively in your client's subconscious?

You can use future pacing in your sales presentation to encourage visualisation of your solution as well as pre-framing any objections that you think may arise after your pitch. By talking about situations that arise in the future and how your product or service will deal with those situations, you are effectively future pacing your prospect.

Typically with future pacing, you would chose three situations and assess the new behaviour at each. It is the same with selling. In a sales scenario, future pacing three times may be a little too many, so stick to one or two.

To future pace a sale, you want to presuppose your solution has been adopted, so ensure to build that presupposition into the question. Here is how a few future pacing questions may look.

- So, once you have installed our new system, how much quicker will you be able to add new users?
- After you have completed our diet and exercise program, how much better will you feel about your holiday photos?
- When you have this new system, how much easier will it be to get the teams working together?

## PUTTING YOUR FBI STATEMENTS TOGETHER

So now you know what comprises a FBI statement, it is your time to make some for yourself. You are going to write an exhaustive list of all of your product or service's Features. Then you are going to take a handful of your key features, and write out 5 generic and immediate Benefits that could link to the feature. Finally, you are going to write out Impact statements for 5 possible values that could drive the purchase of what you are selling.

Make sure you write these out in full and get used to how they link together. Your sales presentation should be fluid and this is the first place you can get in some practice.

### FBI Statements

# OBJECTION HANDLING

No matter how good your sales presentation, from time to time you will face objections.

I know some sales trainers say that if you get it right you shouldn't get any objections, but I am not trying to teach you how to blast through someone to make a sale.

When you are engaged in a healthy conversation with your prospect, they are going to ask you intelligent questions about how your solution fits in with their problem.

- Wouldn't it be better to use a XYZ approach in this case?

- Surely we can do that element in-house?

- We don't really like doing it that way. We got burned before.

Each of these objections is a legitimate concern that your prospect has.

However, if you are able to elegantly help your customer come back round to your way of thinking, they will be even more bought in to what you have to offer them. In fact, immediately after an objection is often the perfect time to ask for the deal.

You need to know the common objections that arise when selling your product or solution and you need to get good at delivering your response. In fact, in this section you will even learn a way to get rid of common objections before they arise.

For the rest of the objections you may face, you need to learn different ways of handling these comments. Because objections will come at you in all shapes and sizes, you need a range of different styles of objection handling methods.

What we will cover in this section is 5 different forms of objection handling, some that are suitable for simple objections and others that are designed to handle even the most difficult and complicated of challenges that can arise.

---

## REFRAMING

Do you see the old woman or the young lady?

A frame provides a context for a given subject matter. Similar to a camera lens focussing on any particular subject at any given time, the frame that you apply to a situation will often determine the interpretation you make.

For example you live in a penthouse apartment (congratulations, aren't you doing well!) and on each side of your apartment you have a different view: a forest, a jail, a lake and a brick wall. However, you are only allowed to have a window on one side of your house. Which do you chose?

If you can only view one of this list from your apartment then the view you chose will impact your opinion of the apartment. Same apartment, just a different view.

Reframing in sales is about changing the frame of an experience. Instead of trying to get a customer to change their opinion about a situation, you simply help them see the same situation through a different frame, through someone else's perspective for example.

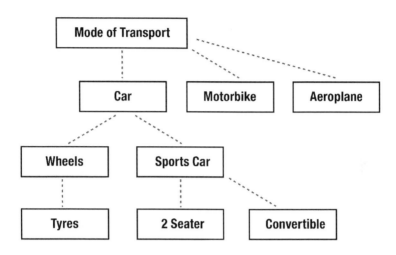

In NLP, there are 2 types of reframe, both of which can be used to handle objections.

## CONTENT REFRAME

In a content reframe, you are attempting to shift the frame of your prospect to a viewpoint that sees the objection in a less difficult light. For example, does someone see the high cost of a product as expensive, or do they see it as a luxury product that not everyone is in a position to own.

**The question to ask yourself and the prospect in this situation is:**

*What else could this mean?*

*What is the positive intention of this behaviour?*

*How else could I describe this behaviour?*

**Below are a couple of Content Reframes for some typical objections.**

It's very expensive!

- We are a luxury product.
- We offer a level of service far above that of our competition.
- Would you want something that everyone else can afford?

You aren't a very big company!

- We are able to give clients more personal attention.
- We are able to respond faster to the needs of our customers.
- We work in a brand new field which is about to explode.

## CONTEXT REFRAME

A context reframe is used to help put negative aspects into a more positive light, not by changing the behaviour, but rather by changing the situation in which that behaviour is used. Remember the presupposition that stated 'every behaviour has a positive intention'? Well, any behaviour can be useful if used in the correct context, but when applied in the wrong context can seem like an objection.

Context reframes work well with objections that say 'I'm too...' or 'I wish we could stop doing...' For example, being too boring is not a great skill to have as an after dinner speaker, but would be great for getting rid of unwelcome guests at the end of a night.

**To apply a context reframe, ask one of the questions below.**

- When would this behaviour be useful?
- Where might this be more appropriate?
- Where would this behaviour be a resource?

**Below are a couple of Context Reframes for some classic objections.**

- It's going to take too long to develop.

---

- We take the time to develop and test our solutions fully.

- It allows our clients to be fully involved in the design process.

- It is a very complicated piece of equipment.

- The features are very advanced and can conduct the most complex tasks.

- Only trained members of staff will want to use this machine.


## PRE-FRAMING

Pre-framing uses the ideas from both content and context reframing, but as the name implies, addresses the objections before they arise. This is a very useful technique to use when you have a product or service that gets a similar objection on a repeated basis.

Objections tend to happen when there is an element of surprise, or when a prospect knows they have a particular question or concern. In a typical sales pitch, these questions may not be answered until nearer the culmination of the meeting. If this is the case, then you may want to consider pre-framing your objection handling statements.

A classic example is that of price. Sales people almost always leave the price until the end of the meeting because they want to build up the value of the offering before revealing the cost (this is a good idea in general!). However, if you are working with a prestige or high level product, you do not really want to unveil a huge price at the end unless the prospect is expecting it. Otherwise, you may be greeted with an astonished gasp, and the sound of someone falling off their chair.

To pre-frame an objection, use one of the reframe methods mentioned previously, and make a statement that puts the inevitable objection into a positive light. Below are a few examples:

- As you know, we only deal with a select few clients who operate at a certain level of business. Our product is not affordable for everyone, which is why we carefully select the businesses we want to work with.

- The timescale for delivery of this product is a lot longer than you are used to. We have found that by extending the design phase, clients are able to have a better final product which is more suited to their business.

- You are probably used to a more flexible working arrangement, but what we have found by getting into a longer term contractual arrangement with clients is that we commit more to the project, giving a stronger end result.

Your challenge is to identify the objections that you get on a regular basis and create a pre-frame statement that will handle those objections before they even arise.


## CHUNKING LATERALLY

As you discovered earlier, chunking helps to move the conversation between the various levels of abstraction, ranging from vague and intangibles values down to the granular detail of the features of your product. However, you can also chunk laterally which is a great technique to create alternative solutions to a problem.

Remember your chunking up questions?

> *What is this an example of?*
> *For what purpose?*
> *What is the intention?*

Each of these will give you the motivation behind a choice or decision. It is a lot easier to reach agreement when you chunk up compared to chunking down. Understanding the motivation will allow you to suggest a solution that is in alignment with your prospect's values.

For example, you are trying to sell a life insurance product to your customer and they are resisting, not comfortable with the decision. If you chunk up and ask 'what is the purpose of this investment?', you will learn that they are looking to provide for their family for when they have gone. Now you understand this motivation, what are all the other products you can sell that will meet this requirement?

- Identify objection around product.
- Chunk up to gain agreement on motivation.
- Chunk down to alternative solutions that meet requirements.

## THE COMING ALONGSIDE STRATEGY

Sometimes when you are faced with an objection, it can seem impossible to handle with even the most cunning of objection handling techniques. The simple reframe method is to straight forward and you find yourself facing what seems like an insurmountable brick wall in the sales process. In these situations, it requires an approach that is a little more sophisticated.

One challenge that I have observed with sales people is that objection handling can quite easily turn into argumentation resulting in debate rather than collaboration to find an agreeable solution. In any such sales situation it is vital to maintain rapport, but how do you do that when you're faced with the challenge of objection that seems so difficult to overcome?

This is where the Coming Alongside Strategy can be useful. This 3-step process allows you to maintain rapport and keep the momentum of the conversation going where other sales people would be halted in their tracks.

For the purposes of explaining how this strategy works, we will use the following objection:

*We already have a supplier for your product/service!*

Let's see how to deal with each of these using the coming alongside strategy.

## STEP 1 - COME ALONGSIDE

The first step is to agree with the prospects. With the objection above, the natural reaction might be to say "BUT I bet they don't A, B and C" which is what your company does. If this is your response, in actual essence what you're really saying to your prospect is that they made a wrong decision. Now, any time you tell someone that they made a bad call, the first thing they're going to do is justify it. We don't want this to happen, as by arguing FOR their decision, they are likely to remember all of the reasons they made the choice they did and strengthen their belief that the decision they made previously was the correct one.

So instead of potentially getting into an argument, we need to agree. Here is how you do it.

*"We already have a supplier!"*

*"Great, fantastic."*
(This buys you a couple of seconds whilst you figure out how to word your response!) *"I'm so happy that you've seen the value in using [insert your product or service] and that you're already using somebody to provide this for you. Let me ask you a question: What three things that they offer you are your favourite element of their service?"*

Now if you ask this question, the customers probably going to respond to you a little strangely and try and maybe wriggle out the question. You have to keep them on track. Make sure you discover those three things and get them talking about why they made the decision to buy. What it was that they bought into? Make a note of these because you're going to want to use this information later.

Your prospect is now in a position now where they feel good, they've been talking about themselves and a decision they made previously. You are probably wondering how are we going to do get to the next point where they start taking our solution into consideration.

## STEP 2 - FOOT IN THE DOOR

If we go straight for the close at this point, we will fall some way short. We need two more steps to cross this gap. We do this by establishing a small gap first and then making it bigger.

If you have ever experienced a double glazing sales person come to your house, you will know what I mean by foot in a door. It's literally where they won't let you close the door because they have got their toes wedged in the way. You are not quite fully in the conversation yet but they are not going away at this point. This provides them just enough time to give you some more of their value proposition and hopefully get you to agree to let them in.

A 'Foot in the Door' question is designed to loosen the element of certainty that your prospect has about their current situation. If you can't wobble the table a little then there is no way you are going to get any further. The question might sound something like this.

> *"Ok, great. It sounds like you made a good choice to use that product or service, but let me ask you a question."*
> (Lead with a compliment to help maintain rapport)
> *"What is it that your current provider doesn't offer that you wish they could?"*

This question forces your prospect to consider the gap between where they are and where they want to be. Notice the use of a presupposition in the question as well.

Now of course, it would be great if your prospect starts listing all of their supplier's faults (and if they do, have some paper ready to make notes!), but the chances are they are not going to answer this directly. If so, you need the seven words to get past ANY objection.

## 7 WORDS TO GET PAST ANY OBJECTION

When you read this technique, you are going to think this is far too simple to work. Surely people are not going to fall for this? Can you get past any objection using just seven little words? Really?

---

The truth is, after a few times of using it, you are going to have to stop yourself from laughing at how effective it can be. Trust me when I tell you that these seven words are potentially the most powerful words you can use. However, before I tell you the words, I have to tell you why they are so good.

Remember the good old double bind close? Which one do you want, the red one or the blue one? Would you like me to visit you Tuesday morning or Wednesday afternoon? We laugh at this type of close now because it seems so dated, and in truth, there is always a third option... saying no! This type of close asks for commitment, and unless someone is sure, getting a decisive answer will be a challenge.

This is where trial closes can be useful. By taking the element of commitment away from the conversation, you are more likely to get a truthful response. Ask your prospect for their opinion rather than their signature allows you to get incremental buy in that will allow you to pitch with confidence towards the end of the sale.

The way trial closing works is by reducing the certainty in the situation by using what I call Watering Down Language. We use these language patterns all the time in language anyway when we want to minimise the impact of our communication. Think about the last time you got into trouble and had to explain it to someone.

> *"Well, you see, it kind of happened a bit like this. I was, you know, just walking along the street when, out of nowhere, this bar of chocolate just jumped into my mouth! I didn't even really chew, but you know what chocolate is like! Anyway, it wasn't really my fault, not 100% anyway. Please will you, well, you know, forgive me?"*

Notice how each of the key points has a lot of fluff around it in an attempt to disguise the actual facts.

So the seven words use both of these concepts in an attempt to bypass the commitment that the response might require. Those seven words are:

> *"If you could, what would you say?"*

If you have never tried using these seven words then you are probably a little disappointed. The longest word in there is only five letters long. You were probably expecting some sort of ancient text uncovered from an Egyptian tomb or at least something that would score high in Scrabble! However, these seven words have the power to get you past any conversational blockage. Let's see these seven words in action.

*"Ok, great. It sounds like you made a good choice to use that product or service, but let me ask you a question. What is it that your current provider doesn't offer that you wish they could?"*

*"Nothing, they are great, no problems at all"*

*"Ok, I know that company and their work really is pretty good, but, if you could, what would you say?"*

*"Well, there is this small issue, and they probably could do this a little more. Come to mention it..."*

It really is that easy. You might find you need to ask this a couple of times with the most stubborn of prospects, and be sure to keep a cheeky smile on your face when you ask this question. However, I promise you that you will be amazed at the power of this question.

Notice how you use a little softening and watering down language before the question. You can also change these seven words slightly if you need to, but make sure you never go over seven words. Other examples include:

*"If you could, what might you do?"*

*"If there was, what would it be?"*

*"If you did, what would you do?"*

If you can find a way to get this down to six words, let me know.

---

If you have asked the foot in the door question effectively, your prospect will start telling you things that they're either not satisfied with in their current provider or they may have a wish list. These responses will be small things that they would like to have a little bit more, but haven't necessarily been important enough to make a change in the past.

Here is your challenge. These little issues alone will not provide enough motivation to create the drive and determination necessary for your prospect to change supplier. You need to make a mountain out of this molehill!

## STEP 3 - KICK DOWN THE DOOR!

Back to our double glazing sales person with their foot in a door. We need to get into the house to give the rest of our sales presentation, so like an action movie, we are going to bring our other foot through and kick the door down. You have just created some doubt and a little bit of an itch. Now it's time to drive a huge wedge into that wound and drive the motivation level through the roof.

Remember, the fastest way to get someone to act is to get them to associate massive, immediate pain to not taking action. We need to extrapolate the minor inconveniences that our prospect has just told us and turn them into significant issues that will have a major impact and cause massive pain. You do it by asking this question:

> *"If you were to continue with the product or service that didn't provide A, B and C,* (the three shortcomings that your prospect gave you) *what would that mean to you?"*

You will likely need to give them time to think about this question. In their mind, your prospect is imagining the future implications of using a product or service that doesn't fully meet their needs or requirements. (If there is a silence as your prospect thinks, avoid jumping in with a second question that is easier to answer. You want your prospect to fully associate to your question and give you a full response.) The full script looks like this:

*"We already have a supplier!"*

*"Great, fantastic. I'm so happy
that you've seen the value in using
[insert your product or service] and that you're already using
somebody to provide this for you. Let me ask you a question.
What are three things that they offer you which are your
favourite element of their service?"*

*"We originally chose them because
of ABC and because we knew that Joe Bloggs
had used it before and had found it worked
well for him. That, and they offered us finance
terms that worked well for us."*

*"Ok, great. It sounds like you made
a good choice to use that product
or service, but let me ask you a question.
What is it that your current provider doesn't
offer that you wish they could?"*

*"Nothing, they are great,
no problems at all"*

*"Ok, I know that company and
their work really is pretty good,
but, if you could, what would you say?"*

*"Well, there is this small issue,
and they probably could do this
a little more. Come to mention it..."*

*"If you were to continue with
the product or service that didn't
provide A, B and C, what would
that mean to you?"*

Eventually, they should give you enough information that you can use to position your product or service in a way that requires them to hear what you have to say. If you have been able to shake their certainty and got them associated to the potential downside of their current situation, they will now be receptive to your alternative.

---

You may find that if your second question, the foot in the door, elicits a response that removes the need for this third question. For example, your prospect replies and then says "wow, I never realised that before", chances are pretty good that they have identified the shortcoming themselves. In these situations, you do not need to ask the third question completely. Instead, you can use an assumptive question that does not require your prospect to answer before moving the conversation along. An example could be:

> *"Ah, so you realise that your current product doesn't offer XYZ.*
> *Well, I know I don't need to tell you the impact that would have*
> *on your business long term, do I?"*

So, to summarise, the Coming Alongside Strategy looks like this:

**Step 1 - Come Alongside** - Maintain rapport by complimenting your prospect's decision and ask for the main reasons that purchasing decision was made in the first place.

**Step 2 - Foot In The Door** - Loosen your prospect's certainty by asking them for some small aspects that are not being fulfilled. Remember those seven words and try not to smile when they work.

**Step 3 - Kick Down The Door!** - Extrapolate these small issues and make them massive and painful so that your prospect is compelled to want to hear your alternative solution.


## PERCEPTUAL POSITIONS

Have you ever been in a situation where, no matter how hard you try, you just can't find a way to get your prospect to come around to your way of thinking? They can only see the problem from their personal perspective and unless you find a way of getting them to change their viewpoint, chances are the conversation isn't going to go much further.

Perhaps you might have experienced a similar situation yourself once before. Have you ever had a problem that was completely unsolvable, something you have been working on for months and months with no success, only to have a friend look at the same situation and give you the answer in a matter of seconds?

It might be nice to get a fresh pair of eyes in those tricky situations with your prospect, but involving someone else at this stage of the sales meeting is never really viable. You will probably have to go right back to the start of the process to ensure the new person is fully on board with you, by which time your chief decision maker is either catching up on some sleep or has picked up the half-finished sudoku puzzle on the corner of his desk.

Instead, we can use a technique called Perceptual Positions to help your prospect develop that fresh perspective themselves without needing a third party. Perceptual positions involves getting your prospect to adopt someone else's viewpoint rather than their own and by picking the appropriate person for substitution, you can help to shape the new perspective in a way which will be favourable for you. We are going to look at two particular ways of using this technique.

## SWAP POSITIONS

The first perceptual position technique is to switch positions with your prospect. This works extremely well if you physically change your location, such as by swapping seats or changing who is writing on the board, but you could also do it on a linguistic basis as well.

Once you have swapped positions, ask your customer (the new salesperson) what advice they would give you (the new prospect) in this situation.

The reason this technique works is because, in many situations, your prospect will know what they need to do, but end up holding themselves back with their own limiting beliefs and negative thoughts arising from their current situation. They may even have some tension arising due to the fact they have a salesperson in front of them trying to get them to buy something.

By getting out of the customer chair and into the position of a sales person coaching them, this frees your prospect up to be more objective with their responses. In this position, you can also ask other questions that might help your prospect come even closer to your way of thinking, such as other possible areas of application, referrals and even the real value of the proposed solution to your prospect.

## TRUSTED ADVISOR

Perceptual positions technique number two involves identifying somebody that your prospect admires and then gaining advice from this new person's perspective.

For example, ask your prospect how they think Richard Branson would approach an advertising campaign that was going up against the industry leader. What advice would Branson give and, if he had to do it all again, how would he do it better?

Alternatively, how would Arnold Schwarzenegger approach taking on a new endeavour. How would someone who went from bodybuilder, to Hollywood superstar to governor of California approach changing careers or a new project?

Your prospect has to know the third party well enough to be able to imagine what their reaction might be like. If they have told you about particular role models then these would be great to use. Otherwise, you can suggest someone well known that would approach the situation in a manner that would support your cause.

For example, Branson was well known for being aggressive in business when everyone else told him to be sensible. Schwarzenegger had no hesitation in moving on from being the best body builder to one of the most famous movie stars of all time to being head of state for one of the most high-profile places on the planet. I am sure you can think of a well known person whose approach to life would support your argument in these cases.

The key thing to know is that, even though you are getting your prospect to think through someone else's point of view, the responses they ultimately give belong to them. By temporarily adopting a new persona, your prospect is able to access a different part of their own personality, a part of them that may have been blocked by the pressure of the given circumstance. Allowing this part to be expressed gives the prospect more freedom of thought and therefore more options to choose from.

Avoid giving the client the advice you know you want them to get. For example, telling them how adventurous Branson was is unlikely to have the same effect as your client coming to the same conclusion. In fact, you telling them is likely to elicit a negative response such as "yeah, well we would all be as brave as Branson if we had his money" and this will not help move the conversation forward.

Can you see how using perceptual positions can be useful in getting your prospects to think differently and come around to your viewpoint? Instead of seeing objections as challenges, you have helped them approach the same problem from different angles and with a different mindset each time. This is a powerful technique for getting your prospect 'un-stuck' in a tricky situation.

## 6 STEP REFRAME

The 6 step reframe pattern in NLP is used to communicate directly with parts of the unconscious mind that have a positive intention whilst simultaneously having a negative impact on the individual's behaviour. Once the positive intention of that part is identified, a more holistic and ecological form of expression can be identified.

With objections, we have a similar situation. As sales people, we must assume that the objection has a positive intention and so if we can work with our prospects to meet the needs of that 'part', we can effectively handle the objection.

Below is how to use the 6 step reframe to handle objections.

### Step 1 - Clarify the Objection

Don't be in a hurry to handle the objections that arise. Spend some time clarifying your prospect's comments to allow you to chunk down into the specifics behind the objection. If the objection is that "it's too expensive", which part of your product or service appears to be more expensive? If the objection is that "the team won't like the new software", why exactly will the team have their reservations? Chunk down and clarify the finer details of the objection you face. The more clearly you have established the objection, the easier it will be to go through the remaining steps.

## Step 2 - Establish Communication with that Behaviour

Here you need to ask your prospect the following question:

*"If you can find a suitable alternative to the objection, would you be open to it?"*

At this stage of the sale, it is likely that most prospects will agree to look for an alternative perspective. Their objection probably does not mean that they do not want to buy your product, rather they want to make sure that they feel fully confident in the decision they are going to make.

In a clinical situation, the communication is unconscious, and you identify or embed a physiological trigger that symbolise a positive or negative response. This requires good sensory acuity skills. In the sales situation, you need to remain aware of your prospect's reaction at each stage to ensure they are giving congruent responses. Don't necessarily just accept the words that your prospect is saying (remember, they only account for 7% of communication!).

## Step 3 - Identify the Positive Intention of the Objection

Remember the presupposition that every behaviour has a positive intent? This is especially true with objections. If somebody does not want to buy your product immediately then there is something holding them back which serves a purpose to them. You need to identify this positive intention and then position your product as one that helps them achieve this goal.

For example, a common objection is that a prospect does not want to buy your product because it's too expensive. Your goal is to uncover the reasoning behind them thinking of your product as expensive. Is it that they want to save money, and they have recently been cost-cutting throughout their business? Do they not recognise the extra secondary value your service offers beyond the immediate benefits because they do not measure success in that way? Are they comparing you to some other related product that they had a bad experience with and want to make sure they are making a good decision? Always look for that second level of objection behind what is actually behind said.

You may find that you need to chunk down and ask more detailed questions to get to the true positive intention of the objection. This is where your rapport skills will also be tested, because asking these kind of probing questions can seem a little invasive. However, they are vital to ask if you are going to successful handle this objection.

## Step 4 - Suggest Empowering Alternatives

Step four is to align your product or service in ways that supports the positive intention of the objection. In a coaching situation, you would ask the client for suggestions on alternative behaviours to replace the existing negative behaviour. When handling this as an objection, your job is to align your product or service in ways that you support the positive intent.

Let's take the above intentions and explore how we would align ourselves.

If your prospect is cost-cutting, explain how your solution can help reduce costs immediately or in the longer term. Perhaps you can emphasise the elements you have included in the overall package that they will not have to purchase separately. Maybe your product increases sales revenue, so you can encourage your prospect to look at the bottom line rather than just expenditure.

Suggesting different measurement criteria for a project can help you get a deal, especially if your service takes time to really shine. If your prospect is thinking short term, expand the timescale and get them to think over a longer scale. You need to know how to justify any secondary benefits of your product, and be prepared to back these up with testimonials.

Making a bad decision is not something many people want to do twice. Be sympathetic and remind the prospect how much they must have learned from their experience, so the chances of them doing the same thing again are minimal. Highlight the money back guarantee you offer, or the reduced tie in periods that you offer new customers.

Lazy method - If you find that you are having to work hard on coming up with these ideas, get your prospect to do the work.

Ask them HOW (presupposition) they would have to view your product or service in a way that makes it appear good value for money. If they can't do it, use perceptual positions and enquire as to how other people in their business might be able to see the benefit. Get your prospect to handle the objection for you by asking a great question and then encouraging them as they start to come up with answers.

## Step 5 - Evaluate the Alternative Options

Step five would be to have them listen to and evaluate these alternative perspectives, either your suggestions or their own advice from their chosen perceptual positions. Do the suggested ways of looking at your product still achieve the positive intention that the original objection was obscuring?

Observe how they react when they take on these alternatives. You may find some incongruence, especially if you have not quite managed to meet the needs of the positive intention, so make sure your sensory acuity is on high alert. Is there any tension or resistance in their body or vocal qualities that might belie the words they are saying?

## Step 6 - Future Pace the New Solutions & Check Ecology

Future pacing allows you to check how well your product or service sits with your prospect moving forward. Think about an example or situation that would arise in the future in which your product would play a key role. Then, ask your prospect how successful this situation would be as a result of the decision they made to buy your product.

In a coaching scenario, you would want to future pace at least three times to ensure the message sinks deep into the unconscious. In sales, you may not need to do this, especially if you get a positive response the first time. However, consider using three scenarios especially if you want your prospect bought into what you are selling them.

This step also allows you to check ecology. Is your solution holistic and beneficial for the whole of the business or your prospect's close circle of friend and family. By emphasising the ecological approach of your product, you are likely to strengthen your relationship and appear less like a salesperson.

The 6-Step Reframe is a great NLP technique for getting people unstuck and helping them to find empowering alternatives to their current behaviour. By getting your prospect to think of different ways to proceed, your prospect is doing the hard work of handling the objection themselves. You don't have to think hard for ways to reframe and change your prospect's mind. Instead, you are helping them get through this restriction themselves, in their own way. If you guide them appropriately, then the end result will certainly be beneficial for you.

## 5 TOP TIPS FOR DEALING WITH AN OBJECTION

### Take your time

By taking your time, you give the impression that you are taking your prospect's objection seriously. Old school sales techniques often suggested ignoring the objection but if you want to develop a relationship with your clients, this really isn't an option. Instead, take a deep breath, consider the objection, then proceed with the most suitable objection handling method.

### Clarify the objection

There is nothing worse than handling an objection perfectly, only to realise you have addressed the wrong objection. By clarifying the objection, you are able to make sure you address the true concern of the prospect, not just the superficial question they may have asked you. For example, 'it's too expensive' might simply mean they aren't able to pay all in one lump sum, but a monthly payment may be a good option.

### Don't waffle

You are close to the sale, so don't get flustered and try to say everything you know to get around the objection. You should know the key objections for your product or service, and should practice all the objection handling techniques until you feel comfortable. Choose your words carefully and deliver them with confidence. Watch the pace of your speech when facing objections as when you get nervous, your speech tends to accelerate.

### Listen! Listen! Listen!

There are many times when an objection isn't actually an objection, more of a rant. In fact, if you just listen and give encouraging looks, you may actually find prospects talk themselves out of their own objections. This is especially true if you have seeded and educated your potential client throughout the sales pitch as when they raise the objection, your previous comments allow them to understand it for themselves.

### Ask a question

Asking a question puts your prospect in the driving seat and gets them to find a solution. Remember, selling is about solving people's problems, not about flogging a load of stuff, so this is a two-way conversation. Ask your prospect what they would do in the same situation, what would make the product work for them or how they might be able to implement it faster than they had any other project before.

## CLOSING

So, you made it to the end of the sales meeting huh? Well done for not getting thrown out before this point. But now comes the difficult bit... closing the sale! All that time and effort you have put in up to this point... better not mess it up now!

This is what many sales training courses are about. I have lost count of the number of times I have been asked to teach closing skills and the various techniques for different situations. However, if you have understood the rest of the book, you will know that the sales close is actually a natural progression from the rest of the conversation.

- Do you need to ask for the business? Yes, absolutely you do.

- Is there a chance they will say no? Yes, this is always a possibility.

- Do you have to face rejection at this moment? Yes, I'm afraid so.

Closing is getting your prospect to commit to the next step of the sales process. In most cases, this will be agreeing to the deal. However, in more complex sales processes, it may simply mean agreeing to the follow up meeting or arranging a technical assessment.

If you have gone through one of the sales questioning models effectively then by the time this moment arises, there will be a natural tension that invites a closing question.

Closing techniques need to be used when this tension does not exist, when there is no internal desire on the part of your prospect to grab your product out of your hands. In these instances, you either need to try and use some form of coercion to convince the prospect to agree to buy. Alternatively you face that awkward moment when you need to ask them to buy your wares but have absolutely no idea if they want it or not.

Closing is all about what happens before that moment rather than what happens in the moment. Do your job well throughout the meeting and you will be able to confidently close anyone. Skip over all the important elements, and you will end up like Aaron.

## ADAM & AARON

One of my highest values in life is health and fitness which means wherever I am in the world, I need to have somewhere to work out. One year, after moving house, I needed to join a local gym. I did a quick search online and found two gyms; one was a top health club, the other the local leisure centre. I decided to visit both.

I arrived first at the high-end club and approached the reception desk.

*"Hi, I'd like to have a look around your facilities."*
*"Do you have an appointment sir?"*
*"No."*

*"Okay, come with me, take a seat and I'll bring somebody out straight away. Can I get you something to drink?"*

My coffee didn't take long to arrive and I enjoyed the relaxed atmosphere and comfortable surroundings. A couple of minutes later, a well-presented young salesperson comes out and introduces himself.

*"I'm Adam. I'm the membership consultant here."*

Rather than getting straight up and showing me around, he started asking me a few questions. How had I found the club? Why I moved to the area? What my interests are and what sort of things I was going to want to do with the club? He asked me a whole range of questions while I drank my coffee, making conversation and getting to know me. Once the coffee was finished, he took me for a tour of the facilities.

We started in the gym, showing me around the machines and equipment and pointing out a couple of interesting features and additional services. We move on to the tennis courts and he let me know about the league which was great for people new to the area who wanted to socialise and meet new people. Then we went through to the swimming pool and he referred back to me talking about triathlons as one of my goals and let me know about the triathlon club that trains each week.

Eventually we get back to the bar area and he asked if he could get me another coffee whilst we discussed membership options. We go over the various packages and then he told me the price: £170 per month. Now at the time, that was a lot of money for a health club membership, but he simply came straight out and said "£170, would you like to join?"

At the leisure centre, I go through the same process but had a very different experience.

Have you ever noticed that a leisure centre reception smells of either one of two things: chlorine or chips? In this case, the reception definitely smelled of fatty chips, a great start to my experience.

*"Hello there, I'm new to area. I'd like to have a look around the gym."*

*"It's up the stairs to the left."*

I don't ever think there was eye contact from the receptionist. I walked up the stairs and found myself faced with another reception. Let's try again.

*"Hello, I'd really like to have a look around the facilities"*

*"Do you have an appointment?"*

*"No, I don't have an appointment."*

*"I'll see if somebody is available, just take a seat over there."*

I headed over to a slightly-too-old leather sofa which had cracked and scratched the backs of my legs (it was summer, I was in shorts, and my leg hairs were getting pulled out like a mini-waxing session!) After a five minute wait, what happened next will remain in my mind forever.

Spiky, but slightly receding hair. A plain white shirt unbuttoned to the naval. Trousers that were slightly too short and most definitely too tight. Finally, shoes so pointed a surgeon could probably use them to perform brain surgery.

*"Hello, I'm Aaron. I'm going to showing you around. Come with me."*

That was it. No coffee, no small talk. Aaron was clearly a man of business. The first place we go to was the gym.

*"This is the gym!"*

Have you ever been shown around a house by an estate agent where all they say is "this is the kitchen, this is the bedroom, this is the garden"? If it wasn't for estate agents the world over, we would probably be putting beds in our kitchens and refrigerators in out bathrooms! This frustrates the heck out of me with estate agents, but it would appear that Aaron had the same sales approach and he pointed out that this was indeed the gym. Then we went through to the pool and I'm sure you can probably imagine Aaron's explanation of the facilities in this part of the building. We go through to the changing rooms and I think that was pretty much it. Back to the lovely leather sofas for the close.

Before we started the tour, I had mentioned to Aaron I had a discounted guest pass for a free 2-week pass that I found in a newspaper. We sat down to discuss the membership prices and come to the actual point of sale. It was a fraction of the price to join, around £30 per month. Adam circled the price on a piece of paper and there followed an awkward silence. He looked at me. I looked at him.

*"Come on Aaron let's see what you've got!"*

As he looked at me and I could see the little bead of sweat running down the side of his head as he knew he had to close me, he had to ask for the sale. Finally, he looked at me and said,

*"So you want to do that guess pass then?"*

Adam did an incredible job. He knew that the club had every single facility that I needed in order to achieve my health and fitness goals. Aaron had no idea. Adam had spent time understanding my challenges, understanding why I was looking to join in your club. Aaron either didn't care or just hadn't got the ability as a sales person. When it came to the close, although Adam had a product that was five or six times the price, he had no hesitation in asking for the sale because he knew that the product he had was right for me. Aaron could only ask if I wanted to join for free for 2 weeks.

Hopefully after reading this true story, you will understand how important the process before closing is to getting the deal. It would have been crazy for Aaron to even try and suggest a package for me and yet how many salespeople do you know that try and do exactly that. This one example highlights the importance of the process of Next Level Persuasion and shows the weakness of any sales methodology that focuses heavily on the close.

However, you do still need to ask for the business, so what do you say?

My recommendation is an assumptive close that explains the next steps. The assumptive close takes away the last opportunity for the prospect to get cold feet and put off making the commitment, and taking the lead by highlighting what happens next helps the client feel at ease at moving forward with you. This kind of close goes something like this:

> *"So Dave, you are probably wondering what happens now. Well the first thing we need to do is get these signed (hand the client the sales paperwork) and once the payment is cleared, we'll get the product in the mail. It normally takes a couple of days to arrive, so why don't we schedule in a time for the end of next week for me to take you through everything. Oh, and how did you want to pay the deposit?"*

Simple, collaborative and supportive. Dave has the emotional confidence and excitement of what happens next and can explain his purchase and the process logically. As you can imagine, this kind of close only works when the person has completely bought into you, your product and the sales presentation which you tailored specifically to their needs. If you try and use this close without following the Next Level Persuasion process, you will experience a lot of resistance. But, follow the process and when you get to this point, hopefully your prospect will be asking you what the next steps are.

However, just in case you want to have a little more flexibility with the kind of close that you use, here is the A-Z of closing techniques with a very quick summary or example of how to use them.

## THE A TO Z OF SALES CLOSES

Alternative Close - *Would you like red or blue?*

Best-time Close - *Emphasize now really is the best time to buy.*

Conditional Close - *So if we can do all that for you its a deal?*

Diagram Close - *So you definitely don't want to be there on the graph!*

Exclusivity Close - *I promise not to work with any of your competitors.*

Fire Sale Close - *Won't last long, everything is going cheap.*

Go On Close - *Oh go on, give it a go...*

Hurry Close - *The faster you talk, the less they think!*

Incentive Close - *If you buy today, you get this bottle of champagne!*

Just In Time Close - *We are lucky to get this agreed before the month end.*

Kids Don't Eat Close - *If you don't buy, my eighteen kids go hungry again!*

Last In Stock Close - *Hurry, you better buy it now before someone else does!*

Mega Bonus Close - *If you buy today, you also get the steak knives...*

No-Hassle Close - *We take care of everything to make it as easy as possible.*

One Time Offer - *Honestly, I have never seen a deal so good!*

Price-promise Close - *So if we can do that same price, we have a deal?*

Quick Call Close - *Let me quickly call my manager to see if we can...*

Rational Close - *Well it seems to make sense and the numbers add up!*

Save-the-world close - *Remember, 1% of what you pay goes to charity!*

Take Away Close - *Actually, this is only for someone who really needs it...*

Ultimatum Close - *Do it now or I'll sell it to your competitor...*

Vanity Close - *Just think how good you will look when you have it!*

When Close - *Two best times to plant a tree? Today or 20 years ago!*

Xebec Close - *Act fast before this ship sails!*

Yes-set Close - *You've agreed to everything so far so do we have a deal?*

Zero Money Close - *You don't even have to pay anything today...*

Understand, however, that these closing techniques should never be substituted for properly following through the Next Level Persuasion sales process. If you feel as though you are having to rely on closing techniques too much, check in and identify at which part of the sales process you are falling short and then make every effort to improve that part of your overall pitch.

# THE ULTIMATE NEGOTIATION FORMULA

Finally, and sometimes even after the deal has been agreed, your prospect may want to negotiate. It is only right that your prospect should want to get the best possible deal and get the most for their money, but as a salesperson, you need to be aware that this may happen and how to work with your client at this point.

Too often, salespeople take the same first step when negotiating, which is to drop the price of a product. However, according to their research, Corporate Executive Board discovered that only 9% of customer loyalty is driven by value-to-price ratio. This means that, although price is an issue, the chance of it driving buying decisions is low.

So if dropping the price is not the solution, what else can we do? This is where the Ultimate Negotiation Formula comes in. Once you figure out what each of the key elements of this formula are and what they mean, you will be able to negotiate and close any deal.

$$V + CI > C + PE$$

## V IS FOR VALUE

This is the benefit and impact of your product or service on the prospect's situation. What is the value of your offering? If your prospect is giving you objections, ask yourself:

**Does my prospect truly understand the value of my product?**

If the answer is no, then you have to do one of three things:

- Develop a better understanding of the values alignment between product and prospect. This may involve questioning your prospect in more detail around what they are looking for from your product.

- When presenting your solution, link back to the prospects values and the impact your product will have on their situation. See the Presenting your Product section for a reminder.

- Offer extra products or service that will support your initial product and add significant value without adding to the cost of the product.

Building the value of your product is what will draw your prospect into it as well as motivate them to take action. The greater the value of your product to your prospect, the more motivation there will be to purchase.

## CI IS FOR COST OF INACTION

Whilst value is a great motivator, it may not necessarily drive immediate action. People are driven by two factors; towards and away from motivation. If you imagine a donkey at the beach, kids sit on its back and get given a carrot on the end of a stick. However, as appetising as the carrot no doubt is, the donkey doesn't get moving until it receives a quick slap on its rump from its handler.

Away from motivation is often a more immediate motivator than dangling carrots. Whilst you can build up away from motivation in the Value section of the formula, highlighting the Cost of Inaction can really help build this driving force.

So what can make up the cost of inaction?

Let's look at retirement investments that rely on the cost of inaction heavily to sell their product. The salesperson may start to paint a picture of what life would be like with no retirement financial planning, the pain of not being able to afford to heat your home or not being able to feed yourself properly despite working hard for over 40 years. They then paint the opposite picture, contrasting the pain of not investing with the relative comfort of having a sensible retirement plan.

Without highlighting the pain points of not taking action, the drive to buy the product would not be there. Think about how Scrooge must have felt in the Christmas Carol, and how it might have been different if he had three nice ghosts visit him and show him what could be good if he changed. There would certainly have been a different result.

## C IS FOR COST

As already mentioned, dropping your price to handle objections is not a good idea. It sets a bad example and may give the impression that you do not value your own product or service highly enough. Also, if you can immediately give a discount, were you offering the best price to start with or were you trying to gain some free extra margin on your product. If you are trying to profit from your prospect in a non win-win context, this may not set the relationship off well.

Finally, never forget that you are in sales to earn commission, and dropping the price effectively gives you a pay cut!

## PE IS FOR PERCEIVED EFFORT

Notice this does not say true effort, but perceived effort. You might think it is simple for someone to start using your product, but in your prospect's head, they are starting to make all sorts of excuses.

- What am I going to do with the old one?
- The staff just got used to that one and it took ages to train them to that level!
- I'm going to have to tell Bob we don't need him anymore!

Unless there is significant value, the perceived effort may outweigh the potential benefits your prospect could get from your offering. However, simply increasing the value may not be enough, unless you remove some of the resistance.

Instead, why don't you try to make it easier to buy your product. Remove some of the effort it would take to start using your service and generally make the whole buying process a lot smoother. For example:

---

- Offer a free installation service and removal of old systems.

- Suggest a free no-obligation trial period to test the product.

- Negotiate credit terms or interest-free repayments.

- Give free training to anyone who will be using the new product.

- Manage the entire migration process and liaise with previous suppliers.

Think now, what changes or additions would make it easier to buy your product or service? Make a list and commit to helping reduce the perceived effort of using you instead of your competition.

So you finally made it to the end of the sales process keeping in mind the mantra "there is nothing worse than premature selling!", but eventually there does come a time to get your prospect to commit to take action and buy what you are selling. However, by this point in the sale, the action step is obvious as you have been educating all the way through the process as to what decision to make. Your prospect is keen to make a decision as you have been motivating right from the moment you started to understand the values behind this purchase. The close, getting your prospect to commit, is therefore the simplest part of the sale. However, there is something about being this close to success that gets your heart racing. Take a deep breath. You have done a great job... now finish it in style.

**Here are some of the main points to take away from this chapter.**

- Remember your solution should be Prescriptive, not Speculative. By this point, you should know exactly what your prospect wants and why they want it. There should be no guess work. Tie your presentation into your prospect's values and they will recognise exactly how perfect your solution is for them.

- If an objection arises, be cool. You know your product inside out and recognise the value it offers, but think back to the first time you heard about it... did you get it straight away? Often it is just the slightest reframe that gets the conversation back on track which is easy with enough rapport.

- Don't be like Aaron... ever! Yes your prospect might say no, but if what you offer them is exactly what they need then who is missing out? Know the value of what you offer, assume that your prospect will want to do business, and then close confidently and concisely, as if you have done it thousands of times before.

- We all want the best deal, and so will your new client. Be prepared to negotiate at the end, but don't think this just means on price. Think of all the other ways that can tip the balance in your favour. If you drop the price this time, there is a good chance it won't be the last time.

# CHAPTER 10
# PURPOSE

| OPENING | CONNECTING | EDUCATING | MOTIVATING | COMMITTING |
|---------|-----------|-----------|------------|------------|

| PREPARING |
|-----------|

| PURPOSE |
|---------|

*"The purpose of life is not to be happy. It is to be useful, to be honorable, to be compassionate, to have it make some difference that you have lived and lived well."*

**- Ralph Waldo Emerson**


*"The mystery of human existence lies not in just staying alive, but in finding something to live for."*

**- Fyodor Dostoyevsky**

The alarm goes off earlier than normal. You remember setting it the night before because you wanted to get a head start today. You slide out of bed silently as the other sleeper must not awaken, head into the kitchen and put the kettle on. As you look outside, the rest of the world sleeps and the only light in the world shines from behind you, casting your silhouette long into the distance. People must wonder what you are doing up at such an hour, themselves preferring the extra hour or two in bed, but for some reason they never ask, they just assume you must be crazy. It's a shame really, because if they did ask, you know the answer you give them would wake up that same intensity within them too.

For most people, the only time they experience this is when they have to get up early to get to the airport and begin their holiday adventures. However, this level of excitement is not reserved for those about to explore distant shores. Instead, it lies in the feeling of anticipation of the greater pleasure ahead. For those people with the sense of being on the right path, every day feels the same as the jet-setting holiday goer.

Having run countless personal development seminars and workshops, I know the question of Purpose in a business context can raise some eyebrows. So many times I have seen professionals decide that, actually, their purpose is not to work but rather meditate above the clouds in the mountains of Nepal. When they begin this period of introspection, they inevitably decide that they cannot realise their purpose within their role and the answer must be 'out there' somewhere, taking time out to travel to the spiritual centres of the world looking for that lightning bolt of inspiration delivered straight from the hand of the divine. They return a more relaxed, care-free individual, but often have no more of a clue about their identity and purpose than they did when they left. However, they do have a cool photo collage on their wall to document the adventure.

> *"Before Enlightenment chop wood, carry water. After enlightenment chop wood, carry water."*
> **- Zen proverb**

I don't want you to quit your job. In fact, there is absolutely no need to if you want to fulfil your purpose. As the Zen proverb above suggests, what you do upon reaching enlightenment is no different to what you did when you were searching. Instead it is your approach to what you do that has changed. In The Way Of The Peaceful Warrior, Socrates says to Dan "You practice gymnastics, I practice everything!" as a way of telling him to approach life in the same way as he dedicated himself to his athletic training.

Before this gets too fluffy I'm going to bring it back to Next Level Persuasion and attempt to explain why Purpose is so important to those people dedicated to achieving success in a sales career. This chapter will remain as 'professional' as possible, but I want to encourage you to dedicate time to understanding more about who you are and why you do the things you do. The insights you gain will be invaluable to every area of your life, not just in relation to being an outstanding sales person and should become part of a lifelong journey of self exploration.

So why is Purpose such an important part of sales and why does it have it's own section in Next Level Persuasion?

Any journey towards significant success takes time and requires experience. If you have ever attempted such an endeavour, you will no doubt have noticed the dropouts beside the path. These dropouts usually come in the form of stories from others that have tried and not achieved the level of success they were initially hoping when they themselves set off. "Oh I tried that once, its tough!" "How can you make those cold calls? I hate them!" "I just couldn't take the rejection after a while!" Most of these story tellers mean well and are simply hoping that their cautionary tales aid in the protection of the would-be salesperson. In reality, their stories of adversity and hardship rarely portray a positive message of the sales profession.

> *"Don't wish it was easier wish you were better. Don't wish for less problems wish for more skills. Don't wish for less challenge wish for more wisdom."*
> **- Jim Rohn**

In life, the only way to achieve success is to push beyond the resistance. Anyone who has ever been to the gym or worked out understand that it is the resistance which causes growth and the person that can endure great amounts of sustained stress and tension will find themselves with the fitness and physique they desire. In the gym, it is the resistance which causes us to grow and develop and each time we work out, we actively seek out ways to make our exercise sessions more challenging and intense.

For some reason, in sales, many people see that same resistance as a reason to get off the treadmill. Instead of welcoming the challenges as opportunities to improve and learn more about selling, they decide that they simply are no good at that element of sales. This limiting belief can easily spiral into a self fulfilling prophecy, leaving the salesperson in despair and rummaging through the job pages as they prepare their cautionary tale to perpetuate the cycle.

*"To live is to suffer, to survive is to find some meaning in the suffering."*
- **Friedrich Nietzshe**

So what is the difference between success at the gym and success at selling? The difference lies in finding a strong enough reason why you are prepared to go through the adversity, face the rejection and spend the countless hours on the phone booking appointments. In the gym, it is easy as we already hold in our minds a picture of our ideal physique and we know that every pound we lift and calorie we burn is taking us, step by step, in the direction of our goal.

Can you imagine what would happen if you treated selling like a workout? In the beginning, you would start by just getting used to the exercises, doing a few sets of cold calling just to see how it feels and not too worried about the outcome. Maybe you experience failure two or three times before moving onto another exercise that works that same body part. In fact, you could probably come up with a whole workout based around prospecting: cold calling, networking events, handing out flyers, giving a talk, attend a trade show. In the gym, after a workout like that your muscles would be super pumped. Take that approach in sales, only moving on after reaching failure a couple of times, and you will certainly notice the difference in your opportunity pipeline.

Gradually, you start progressing in the intensity of your sales 'workouts'. You start approaching the more challenging accounts and prospects, confident in the knowledge that you have progressed so far up until this point and this is the next challenge for you. You may fail early on, as you might also in the gym when you make that jump. However, you know that if you continue with the same persistence and determination that has brought you to this point, this too will one day seem easier.

This is where Purpose comes into play. Your purpose is your meaning in the suffering. It is why you do what you do. If your purpose is strong and clear then nothing will be able to stop you from reaching your goals. Sure there may be things that slow you down or try and knock you from your path, but in the end, you have that internal drive that will keep you going no matter what.

So how can we start identifying our purpose? Firstly, you need to know it is comprised of two main elements:

- Know what you want;

- Know why you want it.

The first part is easy and we have already discussed goal setting in this book as part of the Preparing stage of Next Level Persuasion. However, the goals in your purpose are usually higher level, longer term goals.

For example, a simple goal might be to buy a sports car or to go on a lavish holiday. However, when you get into your sales activities, it would be easy to justify not picking up the phone by saying to yourself 'I don't really need the leather seats' or 'I'm sure 4-star is just as good as 5-star".

A goal that is part of your purpose, therefore, needs to keep you focused and not allow you that escape route. How do you think you would approach selling differently if your goal was to pay your parents mortgage off before you reach your 30th birthday or to save enough money to send your children to a private school or university? With these more significant goals which both carry significant emotional weight, the urge to relax and take things easy will still exist, but there will be an even more significant reason to persist.

You might argue that passion will do the same thing, an exuberance that motivates and excites and inspires, and you would be right to a point. But let me ask you a question. Have you ever set a new year's resolution? You see, passion gets you started and will make things happen at a million miles per hour initially. But what happens at that first bump, or challenge, or plateau? Passion stays ignited when everything is going well, but tends to fade over time. The reason most people don't stick at their new year's resolutions is

---

because they don't have a good enough reason why they want to do something. Passion gets you started, but Purpose will keep you going.

Once you are clear on the things you want, you have to tie that to your values and why you do the things you do. As you will now know from the chapter on Motivating, every one of us has a different set and hierarchy of values that determine the actions we take and the decisions we make in a given context. If you went through the exercises and wrote out your own values, you will already have an idea of what is important to you in your own life. The way to check whether your life is a true reflection of what you think your values are is to look at the actions you take each day. For example, someone that says they value health but sits on the sofa all day eating pizza may not really value health that highly.

To help you define your purpose, it is helpful to know how your values were formed in the first place and how you can re-create them to serve you better moving forward.

We form a lot of our character during our early years. Sociologist Morris Massey describes three major periods during which values are developed: the Imprint period, the Modeling period and the Socialization period.

The Imprint period takes place over the first seven years of our life and, lacking a developed critical faculty, involves us absorbing the events in our surroundings and environment, helping us create our models of the world. Over the next seven years, in the Modeling period, we start to model people we admire, taking on their traits and behaviours and trying them on for ourselves. The Socialization period takes place over the next seven years and sees us taking on some of the personality elements of our peer groups and those people we spend most of our time with.

You are therefore made up of a mixture of all of the different elements of your history, and involved in this is the development of your values which contribute to your purpose. Effectively, you become a combination of the role models you had as a young person. Whose posters did you have on the wall when you were younger? Can you see how they have played a part in who you are today?

Your past goals were likely influenced by the values you developed growing up. If you grew up around successful people, the chances are good that you have success high up on your values hierarchy and so you will likely have set yourself lofty and challenging goals. If your past saw you spending time with a lot of people, you will likely have ensured that your life was also filled with plenty of socialising, possibly spilling over into your choice of job role.

In a similar way, if you were to choose the goals that make up your purpose, these would also likely reflect your current values. People with a strong sense of family will likely have a desire to provide for their children or their parents. Those with a focus on their community will likely want to contribute in a way that supports those they are close to, perhaps by building a school or donating to their church.

Before you jump in and select your purpose based on your past, you need to understand two important elements.

Firstly, your values change as you go through life. Just as your development happens in stages when you are young, so too does it continue into old age. You do not stop changing once you have gone through those first three periods of your life. Instead, all of the people and events that occur in your life continue to shape and mould you each and every day. Highly emotional events tend to be particularly important, such as the death of a close relative or a near death experience, as the global beliefs that are formed in those moments tend to stay with us for a long time.

Secondly, just as your values can be influenced by what happens to you, so too can you affect those events to create the values you wish to be important. If you think about the formative processes you went through when you were younger, you can create the same conditions now that will allow you to re-wire yourself and realign your values hierarchy. Of course, this will not happen overnight, having taken you twenty one years the first time around. However, if you persist and use the following ideas to positively re-program yourself, you will find that the rest of your life changes accordingly.

You are starting to get even more of an understanding now into the importance of values and how they drive decision and action. This detailed knowledge will help you even further when dealing with your clients and prospects as you try to understand how and why they make the decisions that they do. Now let's put that information into action and start to design your purpose, and to do that, we go through three steps.

**Step 1** - Clarify Your Values

**Step 2** - Design Activities To Reinforce Values

**Step 3** - Recognise & Reward

## STEP 1 - CLARIFY YOUR VALUES

This is your opportunity to decide upon the life you want to create for yourself. You have already elicited your own values hierarchy around life, although I would highly recommend you to do so again now. The more times you go through this process, the better you understand the process itself. In addition, you will recognise the challenges with answering some of the questions, allowing you to coach your prospects through the same points in your sales meetings. For this process, I am going to assume you have your written values hierarchy in front of you.

As you look down the list and imagine all of the decisions that person would make in each context of their life, ask yourself - Is this the person I want to become?

Believe me, there is no right or wrong answer to this question. Who you are today is made up of the decisions you have made in the past and rarely do we get them all right. If you look at your values and look in the mirror and know that you want to make some significant shifts then this is your opportunity to design the life that you want to lead. Rarely do people ever ask themselves this question, preferring to allow momentum and habit to dictate the way they live their life. As Tony Robbins says 'the past does not equal the future'. Who you are today is the result of your past decisions which cannot be changed, but who you become tomorrow is decided right here, right now.

So look again at your values hierarchy and decide on which values you want and in what order you want them to appear. How do you decide which values you want to have as part of your Purpose? By answering the following questions, you will get some indication of what needs to be important in your purpose-driven life.

## WHO ARE YOUR ROLE MODELS?

I'm guessing you don't still have posters on the wall of your favourite band, but there is a good chance that you still unconsciously model others that you admire. Check your bookcase - whose biographies do you have on the shelf? Whose blogs do you visit regularly online? Who do you move mountains for to see them speak in public?

You can find role models for every area of life, and even if they don't have the complete package, you can certainly take elements from each person to help you design your ideal values structure. For example, who do you admire that is successful in business? From what you know about them, which of their values helped them achieve this level of success? If you adopted these values as your own, what kind of an effect do you think it would have on your results?

Take a moment to list the people that inspire you. Write a list of the values they exhibit that contribute to the results you admire and decide whether you want to include these values in your own personal list.

## WHAT WOULD YOU TELL THE GRANDCHILDREN?

This is what I call the rocking-chair test (although I haven't seen a rocking chair in years, it is how I imagine myself when I get to that age). You are sitting in your rocking chair out on the porch, admiring the view as your grandchildren run amok in the garden in front of you. Suddenly, all of the grandchildren rush up to you and want them to tell you a story about your life, something amazing. What story would you want to tell them?

The key here is not to think about what you have already done, but instead about the most amazing stories you would love to be able to recount. If we look back from a position where the events have already happened, the 'reality' filter does not limit our dreams and ambitions. If you were to imagine these stories today, it might be impossible to see how they would happen, causing you to push those dreams to the side in favour of something a little more 'sensible'. However, when you are telling the grandchildren your story, they don't want to hear sensible, they want spectacular!

The stories you want to be able to tell them likely tie into values you have yet to tap into fully. For example, if you wish you could tell them about a boat trip along the Amazon but you don't even have a passport, this might suggest that travel and adventure are not as high on your current values list as you may like them to be.

Imagine the stories you would like to tell and then consider the values that they represent. Make a list of these values and decide which of these you definitely want to contribute towards your purpose.

## THE EULOGY SPEECH

Many people don't get to hear their eulogy, but imagine if you could. Hiding at the back of the room you get to listen to the stories that people tell about you, your life and the impact you had on them personally. One by one people take the stage and give everyone in the room a small insight into the life that you lead.

What would you want others to say about your life and how you lived? If you heard these speeches today, would they reflect a life you could be proud of? Think of all the different hats you wear throughout your life and the roles you play in different people's lives, what would they say about you as a family member, relationship partner, colleague and friend?

Now imagine what you would like people to say about you. What is different? How would you need to live your life differently in order for people to see you that way? What values would you need to prioritise in order to live that kind of life? Make a list of these values and then decide which are important enough to make it onto your final list.

## THE FIGHT CLUB TEST

There are a couple of scenes in this movie which serve a similar purpose and go some way towards identifying core values. At one point, Tyler is driving a car along a motorway and takes his hands off the steering wheel before asking 'Guys, what would you wish you'd done before you died?', to which the replies were paint a self portrait and build a house. The other notable scene related to this topic was when the two main characters drag a convenience store worker out behind the store and confront him about why he isn't studying to be a veterinarian. At the end of the scene, Tyler says 'Tomorrow will be the most beautiful day of Raymond K. Hessel's life. His breakfast will taste better than any meal you and I have ever tasted.'

Although these two situations may seem a little extreme, they do have a way of getting to the heart of the matter very quickly. Often we give answers to questions that we think society wants to hear rather than the response that we really feel deep inside. By not expressing our true feelings, we end up censoring our own life and end up with an existence that is not what we truly want to experience. These two scenes are a strong reminder that we only get one life and we should not allow things to get in the way of who we truly want to become.

If someone asked you what was the one thing you want to experience, or do, or accomplish, before you die, so that on your last day on earth you feel satisfied and have no regrets in that area, what answer would you give? The values that this response reflects definitely need to feature on your hierarchy.

Now that you have answered each of these questions, you should now have a comprehensive list of the values you would like to feature in your life. Look through your list and imagine living with more of each of those values filling the days of your life. What kind of impact do you think that would have on you?

If you really got your creative juices flowing during that section, you might find you have a huge list of values by the end of the process. Although as humans we are complex creatures and each of these will play its part in our motivation and decision making strategies, on a conscious, pro-active level, it is difficult to keep more than 10-12 in mind on a consistent basis. Therefore, I want you to do what you can to condense the list. Combine values that are similar in nature or maybe delete some that maybe aren't really that important to you after all. Create a concise list of values that you want to have in your life.

Finally, you need to put these values into order. To make it easier for you, all you need to do is chose your top three out of the list and these will be the core values you live your life by moving forward. Look through your list and ask yourself this question:

*If I wanted people to describe me in three words, what would they be?*

As you go through the list, notice the words and values that jump out at you. All of these words are important, but if you only had three to describe you, which of these values would you wish them to be?

At last, you are left with a list of values with three core values at the summit. As you read through each of these words one by one, take a moment to imagine how your life would be if these values were to be expressed consistently. Would the decisions this person makes allow you to live a life full of purpose and passion?

If you have answered honestly and from your heart in all of the previous scenarios, the list of values you have in front of you should represent your ideal image of yourself. All you need to do now is create that person.

## STEP 2 - DESIGN ACTIVITIES TO REINFORCE VALUES

Remember, the measure of a value's true importance is how much of your resources (money, time, energy) you invest into it. This means that no matter how many times you say something is important to you, unless you are acting on it, then it isn't really a value, more of a response that you think society would approve of.

Many of the values on your new list will likely have already existed in the past and so you are probably already acting in accordance with these values. Success was already probably on your list as otherwise I don't imagine you would have read all the way through a book on how to improve as a salesperson, so in this case, you probably have an idea how to realise this value in your life. However, for those new values on your list, figuring out exactly how to invest your resources can require a little creativity.

What you have to remember, however, is that at this point, we are not trying to get our resource allocation completely perfect. Instead, what we are attempting to do is fool our brains by immersing ourselves in our new values until our psychology is re-programmed with our new set of values. This means that all you need to do is think something will help realise one of your values and you will have begun the process. Of course, you can always improve things at a later date, but for now, just allow your ideas to flow.

I am sure you have heard the term 'fake it until you make it'? Well, that is exactly what we need to do in order to re-wire our values. Remember, values drive all our decisions, often unconsciously, so if we are going to begin the re-programming process, we need to make new decisions, especially around how we allocate our resources. However, as we are not yet at the point of being unconsciously able to make these decisions, we need to make very conscious decisions on what we are going to do.

Take one of your core values, ideally one that is new to your list. How are you going to create a life which features this value as one of the core driving forces in your purpose and motivation? Hopefully you can think of a number of different activities that would reflect this value, but the chances are you are not doing any of them as yet, otherwise this value would already have been part of your hierarchy. Instead, you are going to have to do things that you would not naturally have done so that you can really live true to that value. Eventually, these decisions and actions will become second nature as your new values and identity begin to merge with your personality, but until then, you just have to put in the extra effort.

As you can see, changing your values hierarchy will have a significant impact on your future as all decisions made from this point on will have a different focus. Therefore, changing your values should not be taken lightly and for any such change, you need to consider the ecology of your decision as well. Pushing success to the top of your list but letting health drop off might be fine in the short term but will probably not be sustainable, at least without consequence. Keep this in mind when we decide on the new activities you want to undertake.

Also, as we want to keep a strong focus on integrating your purpose into your sales career, you need to think of ideas that allow you to incorporate your new values into your work. Let's say philanthropy and charity have moved into your core values. Instead of taking the rest of your life out and volunteering to work in your local charity shop, how can you realise this value within your role? Perhaps you could commit to donating a proportion of your commission to charity. Maybe you could arrange a sponsored event for the whole of your sales team to be part of which would raise far more than you could do on your own. Your management team may even allow you to support charities within the organisation by providing work placements for young people or those trying to get back into a job.

Whatever values you have, I am sure you can think of a number of ways to realise them within your sales position. As I already mentioned, too many people look outside of their job to find happiness, and in many cases jobs are so restrictive that this may be the only way. However, being in sales gives you that extra element of freedom, assuming you are hitting your targets along the way.

So, now, take your pen and paper and write out your three core values followed by the rest of your values. Then, what I want you to do is write out as many different ideas for activities that will help you experience more of each of the values. Think of examples both inside and outside of your role and your challenge is to see how many different activities you can come up with. Normally, if I am creating such a list, I try to come up with 20 different ideas for each value, which will certainly take some time. However, by the end of this process, you have a number of ideas, some good and others terrible, but by pushing that extra little bit, you will likely come up with some great ideas, especially once you really get creative.

Once you have created each of these lists, pick the activities that you think will make the most impact. Perhaps some activities tick a number of the values. For example, attending a business networking event could help with overall success, allow you to be more social, increase your network of contacts and help you get over your fear of speaking in public. In these cases, I would highly suggest incorporating these in your new monthly routine.

Remember that the test of a value is how much of your resources you invest into it, so when you are choosing your activities, ensure that they reflect your desired value hierarchy, rather than just the activities you think you will enjoy the most. Your core values should have more time, money and energy invested into them than the rest of your hierarchy.

Finally, as you look through this list, imagine what your life will be like now, living with those new values, making different choices and taking on new activities. As you imagine, notice how applying this approach impacts you as a salesperson, how you take on your role, how you talk to clients differently and how they respond differently to you. Think about the impact these changes will have on your level of success and how your commission cheque continues to grow month on month as you live a life on purpose.

## STEP 3 - RECOGNISE & REWARD

There is a force in the universe that recognises when you are on the right path. You will have experienced this before, either on the right side of it or on the wrong side. When you are on the wrong side of this force, everything seems difficult. It seems like nothing is working, you are struggling to get results and what you do get out has absolutely no reflection on the amount of effort you put in to get there.

On the flip side, there are times when it seems that everything is going great and you only need to think of something and it happens, just like that. At these times, you get rewarded for every drop of effort you exert, and working doesn't feel like a chore, it is just what you do.

In psychology, this state is known as Flow. Flow, a state described by Mihaly Csikszentmihalyi, is a feeling of energised focus based on being immersed in an enjoyable activity and it happens when your skills, mindset and emotions are all aligned. This is the same set of criteria as living your life on Purpose. Basically, when you get your Purpose sorted, things are going to start going your way.

Rewarding your progress is something fun to do, but also it will accelerate your development. Positive reinforcement will strengthen your new behaviours, meaning your mind will want to do these things more in the future. As you are effectively trying to re-program twenty-one years of conditioning, you need to do what you can to expedite the process.

There are some things that are really easy to reward. For example, if you decided to stop smoking, you could save up all the money you used to spend on cigarettes and buy yourself something nice each month instead. However, how do you reward yourself for taking your education more seriously and reading a book a week for a month?

Well, in reality, you don't have to do anything too extravagant, just enough to say to yourself that this little treat is to recognise all the effort you have been making. Take your partner to dinner and order a bottle of wine from the bottom of the list rather than the top. Upgrade your next flight rather than sitting in economy class as usual. Take a visit to your favourite shop and buy something that reflects your hard work and latest successes.

Whatever you do to reward yourself, do it regularly and do it gladly. Not only does the positive reinforcement accelerate your adoption of your new values hierarchy, but also indulging yourself raises your own self-expectations. Once you have experienced a few of those finer things in life, you won't want to go back and so this will further strengthen your resolve to become the best salesperson you can be.

As for recognising whether you are living on purpose, you will probably be able to answer this fairly easily you are honest with yourself. However, below are a few external clues in case you are unsure of the answer.

### You wake up with great new ideas every day

At times like this, it pays to keep a notepad by the side of the bed, just in case these flashes of inspiration happen in the middle of the night. Somehow, these new ideas keep popping into your head. A new way of prospecting. A different target market that no-one has thought of. A way to book twice as many meetings in half the time. When you are on Purpose, your creative energy starts to flow!

### People ask you how you do what you do

When you are on Purpose, people will notice, and when the results start coming in, they are going to want to know what you know. You might not even know how to explain it (this will likely get them nice and frustrated), but you just know that since discovering how to align with your Purpose, everything seems to be slotting in together. However, if that answer doesn't land, just tell them you are prospecting really hard.

**People start promoting you even without asking**

You have probably been asking people for leads and contacts for years, but now, all of a sudden people are talking about you, and not in a bad way. People will recognise not just your new levels of success but also your approach to work and life and this will attract them to you.

**Challenges don't feel like such a challenge**

The cancelled meeting. The person that swears at you when you call their office. The lack of staples in the stationary cupboard. These things used to annoy you, but now they don't really matter. Your focus is solely on your positive goals and whilst these little hiccups may be annoying, they don't take your energy or distract you from what you know needs to be done.

**You cant believe they pay you for this**

You enjoy each day so much, you almost feel guilty for taking a salary. All of your values are being met each and every day and you are growing and contributing on a regular basis too. If you had to write out your perfect job, it probably wouldn't get much better than this. However, never let your manager in on this little secret.

# CHAPTER 11
# CONCLUSION

I wish I could see the look on your face right now. Being a salesperson is about pushing people off of the fence that they may be sitting on, getting your prospect to commit to a yes or no answer. As a trainer, I am effectively selling you on new ideas and information that have the potential to improve your sales performance, and just as a salesperson, occasionally this causes me to face rejection. Some people like these new ideas whereas some people don't. Perhaps they don't want to change or don't see the need to change, but with Next Level Persuasion, the big resistance comes when people are forced to look at themselves and how they come across when communicating.

There are countless sales models that have been created, and all of them work because they are built around the similar principles of asking questions, establishing needs and proposing a solution that meets those requirements. Next Level Persuasion is no different in that regard, and yet, there is something within that allows salespeople at every stage of their career to improve and benefit from the lessons.

The difference between Next Level Persuasion and other sales training is not in the process but in the understanding that lies beneath. Selling is not about ticking off boxes on a checklist, it is about connecting with the person in front of you, getting to understand them and then working together to find a solution that your customer feels confident will deliver on their requirements.

The success of Next Level Persuasion doesn't come from knowing the step, it comes from understanding what needs to happen from a psychological standpoint. Having this knowledge enables you to know what is going on in your prospect's mind and then react in an appropriate way that will develop your relationship. If we look through the Next Level Persuasion sales process now, at the end of the book, you will be surprised at how well you understand the underlying principles that accompany each step.

If I asked you about Opening and asked you to put yourself in the position of the prospect, what would you need to know immediately before you would agree to continue the conversation? What would the salesperson have to say that would make you feel confident in their abilities to help you solve your problem? Now you understand what the customer wants you to say, just say it. Use the frameworks like the 4-Mat model to help shape your introductions and elevator pitches and make sure your cold calling uses some kind of pattern interrupt to ensure you aren't just treated like all the other calls that gatekeeper gets that day.

Now you know everything there is to know about Connecting, you will probably never think about your body language again. Instead, your mind is looking for ways to create a deeper level connection by truly trying to understand your prospect, rather than just trying to find superficial things in common that help to break the ice. You also start noticing different things in language, not just the words, but the predicates that give you an indication of the type of person you are dealing with and their preferences for communication. As you get more experience, you will quickly be able to put your own preferences aside and adjust the way you communicate to be even more effective.

I also hope that you realised that the Educating phase is not all about talking, but involves asking questions that get your prospect to come to the realisations themselves. By questions, we aren't just talking about open and closed questions, as now you understand so many more different language patterns that will allow you to drive your prospect's imagination in the direction you want it to go. You ask great discovery questions that allow you to learn more about your prospect, and you ask precisely-worded positioning questions that help your soon-to-be client understand exactly what they need in order to be able to make the right decision for them. You also realise that the answers you get are not always the whole picture, but a reflection of our human tendencies to delete, distort and generalise all the information we have to process and you know the appropriate responses when you don't get quite the answer you want.

As much as the logical information from educating is important, you now know that you can't make a sale without Motivating as well. All the way through your sales conversation, you constantly notice values in your prospect's language and try to understand which of these values will be most important when it comes to making the final decision. After all, values and their hierarchy determine every decision we make and so once you understand how your prospect is wired, you will know exactly how to align your product and service in a way that appeals to them.

Finally, you understand that making a decision, any decision, can be intimidating and so you understand what goes through your prospect's mind when it comes to Committing. You ensure your product presentation is delivered in a way that connects with your prospect's communication preferences and is aligned with their core buying values. If any objections arise, you know that these are just questions in your customer's minds because they can't quite see your proposal from your perspective yet and so you find a way to reframe it for them. When it comes to the close, you already have your prospect in a motivated position, ready to take action, so all you need to do is not be like Aaron.

If you want to know what really makes you a powerful communicator, it is not the words but the energy behind the words that really shines through. If you are 100% in alignment with everything you say and are genuinely interested in the ongoing success of your customer, they will feel this. Something in their gut will tell them that you, above all salespeople, have their best interests at heart and this will create a level of trust that will enable you to reach great success in your career. To do this, you need to have the right underlying mindset, stemming from the beliefs you have about yourself, the world and selling in general. This will determine how you approach the world and the people in it. However, the power comes from your integrity and your alignment with your purpose. If the whole of you shows up at the sales meeting, not just a part of you that you send out to work, you will connect like never before. Don't go out there and be a generic, watered-down version of yourself. Instead, know who you are and what makes you unique and bring that personality to everything you do.

As you graduate from this stage of Next Level Persuasion and start to incorporate these lessons into your sales process, there are a few different ways you can continue to use this book as a resource.

- **Truly mastering each of the techniques in this book will take time** and I suggest you don't try to adopt each of the techniques right away. When you learn to drive, your instructor starts by taking you to a quiet road to teach you the basics, and even helps out a little on the pedals if required. Gradually, they introduce new aspects to driving such as other cars, greater speeds and tricky manoeuvres. This allows you to become comfortable with each element before moving onto the next. I recommend a similar approach with Next Level Persuasion. Pick a couple of techniques and practice them over and over until they become second nature. Once you feel comfortable, move onto the next.

- **Use this book as a self diagnosis tool for improving elements of your sales process.** If you know that there is a particular part of your sales process that needs attention, turn to that chapter and identify a couple of the tools that will make a difference. If you are going to do this, however, remember that you can't just jump to the end. If you aren't closing enough deals, you need to know how to diagnose the problem rather than just blaming it on not enough closing techniques. If you hear 'maybe' a lot, chances are you haven't motivated your prospect enough. If they say 'oh, this isn't what I was expecting' then maybe you need to consider how you are opening the conversation at the beginning.

- **Share the ideas with your fellow salespeople.** There are three levels of knowledge: knowing, knowing and doing, knowing to teach. A lot of people know the facts but never do anything with them. Action sets the people who mean business apart from the rest. Finally, teaching requires a deeper understanding of the information so that you can effectively communicate it to others. By teaching others these ideas, you have to develop your understanding to the next level which, as well as 'paying it forward', ensures that you reach your full potential as a salesperson.

I guess now we are at the end of the book, I have a little confession to make. Part of the reason this book contains over ten years of research is that it has taken me that long to figure out how to write this book. Sitting and typing out the words was the easy part. What took the time to figure out was how I was going to write a sales book that also ticked one of my other major passions in life which is personal development and helping people to improve their lives.

When I was thinking about the structure of the book, I looked at other books in the self help field that inspired me and thought about how they got across their message. Many of the best selling books in that genre use metaphors and stories to embed their message behind the superficial events that take place within. Others break down the challenge at hand into ten steps or seven days or one minute chunks that allow you to dip in and out when you get the chance. I knew I wanted to write a book that helped people change their lives, but I knew, at the same time, it had to be the best sales book I could write. Figuring out this balance took a while... actually it took years.

Then I remembered something. I looked back at all of the sales trainings I had conducted over the years and the sort of results my students had gone on to achieve, and what made me proud was not just the sales numbers they had gone on to reach, but rather the other impacts I had been able to make on their lives.

You see, the techniques contained within this book are not sales techniques, but I'm sure by now you have this all figured out. Instead, the content is an in depth exploration of human psychology and communication, it just so happens that is a very close match with sales. However, you could apply every single one of these techniques in a different context and also get incredible results.

Imagine using reframing when having one of those 'heated conversations' with your partner, and I'm not just talking about bringing them around to your way of thinking either. Being an expert reframer allows you instantly understand any situation from another's point of view which will allow you to de-escalate almost any situation that arises.

How about parents that are able to understand the values of their children and who know how to tie their agenda into what the child wants? I can't remember how many times as a child I was asked to tidy my room. Imagine, however, if you taught an aspiring young sports person about how immaculate their idol's locker was. Do you think it might be easier to do this than shouting or sending them to their room?

Ultimately, however, we are all salespeople. You may not be selling a tangible product, but remember, sales is about getting someone to do something that you want them to do whether they realise they want to do it yet or not. Any time you want someone to do something, you need to sell them on your idea. If you are a teacher, you need to sell your students on the the reason why they need to know the information you can give them. Lawyers have to sell juries on why their argument is more convincing than that of their opposition. Politicians need to sell their constituents on their ideas for their region and why they are best placed to deliver on those promises.

Even if you are in customer service, you should be selling. I once designed a specialist customer service sales training program for a telecommunications company which looked at how their telephone operatives could add extra value by offering elements that would improve usability. Can you imagine being offered ways to make something you bought even better? What would happen if you bought a remote control car as a Christmas present but weren't offered the batteries by the assistant? If you find yourself in this position, think about how you can add value to the already excellent job your sales person has done.

Anyway, I just went off on a bit of tangent (this happens a lot in the live trainings!).

The reason I eventually wrote the book this way is because I realised that I did not have to write a 'self help' sales book, and that by teaching these concepts under the guise of sales I would still be able to have the same impact I desired. When my students told me about their improvements in their relationships, or how they had stopped smoking or how they had taken the general success principles and applied them in other areas of their life, this gave me as much excitement as hearing about their latest deal or how they managed to break their company's sales records.

When I am teaching live, I love to go off on tangents. I find these brief interruptions allow my students to ask the 'what if' questions that allow them to discover the alternative applications, either in the group environment or even just in their own mind. I have tried to build some of this element into the book, but I also know that as you start thinking beyond sales, you will see more applications for the lessons within this book. When you start using the Next Level Persuasion techniques in all areas of your life, that is when you know you have begun to master the techniques and they have now simply become part of how you communicate. You reach the level of unconsciously competent and the art and science of influence and persuasion is now a permanent part of you.

I hope that by reading this book you reach unparalleled levels of success in sales and that success overflows into all areas of your life.

I take a lot of these ideas for granted now, and it is difficult to remember the time when I didn't know these ideas. However, I can still remember the day I began my journey of discovery when a random stranger (now one of my best friends) handed me an audio program by Tony Robbins. Little did I know that one little CD would begin a journey that would completely reshape the rest of my life and be the start of a ripple that would go on to impact thousands of salespeople across the world.

I recently met up with one of my earliest students for a coffee. He is now in charge of a sales team, having been successful as a salesperson and ambitious to progress, and was keen to discuss ideas on how to get his team firing on all cylinders. As he walked towards me, I recognised the smile even though both our faces had gotten a little older. We shook hands, grabbed a coffee and then spent time going over the past ten years, where it had taken both of us and the entire rollercoaster ride that is life.

Then he started telling me about the culture he was building within the organisation, a culture that ties employee success in with personal success. He told me about his dreams of creating a team of salespeople so successful that everyone in their industry would want them on their team, but a culture so strong that nobody would have any reason to leave. He told me about how they all discussed their goals and ambitions and then encouraged each other to succeed, not just to hit their numbers for the month but to really enjoy the life they were creating for themselves each day.

We concluded the meeting and as we walked to the station together, he reminded me of some of the lessons outside of Next Level Persuasion that I shared with him on his training: the principles of success, time management, planning and all of the other elements that go into being a successful person, not just salesperson (and enough content to fill another whole book). He said that for the past ten years, he had been living by those ideas each and every day and owed his success to the way he lived his life. The way he said thank you reminded me of how powerful all of these lessons can be to the people who put them into practice. A couple of days later, as a reward for his success in using them that he was off diving in the Maldives.

If you really apply the lessons of Next Level Persuasion, your ability to communicate will go far beyond that of being a great salesperson. Just like when my friend gave me that CD, I hope that this book starts a ripple effect of success in your life and that flows over into every area of your life. When we meet at a live event or for coffee in the future, I look forward to hearing your stories on how Next Level Persuasion made a difference to you, your results and everyone around you.

For now, commit to being the very best salesperson you can be. Double your resolve to shake off rejection and keep moving forwards towards your goals. Sales is the vehicle that will help you reach your goals of wealth and success and it is now your job to make sure that that vehicle matches your personality for the rest of the journey. And remember, every sale you make is the beginning of ripples in the pond for your customer. Good luck!

> *"I firmly believe that any man's finest hour, the greatest fulfillment of all that he holds dear, is that moment when he has worked his heart out in a good cause and lies exhausted on the field of battle - victorious."*
>
> **- Vince Lombardi**

# ABOUT THE AUTHOR

**Dan Storey** is a NLP Trainer and Master Practitioner who has been training sales people in how to use these techniques for over ten years. During this time, Dan has trained sales people across Europe from almost every industry, including IT, finance, advertising, health and fitness, education and, believe it or not, even exotic dancing.

During this time, Dan has experimented with the best ways to practically use the techniques of NLP in sales situations, as well as how best to train this to sales people of all abilities. Having been in sales situations right from C-level board presentations through to telephone and retail sales, Dan understands exactly what it takes to be successful in sales at all levels. It is this experience that forms the basis of *Next Level Persuasion*, comprising the very best in techniques required to close deals of all sizes.

Dan has been fortunate enough to work with some of the world's top NLP trainers during his career, helping devise the sales processes that lead to millions of dollars in sales over a weekend training programme. Not only that, but having spent years in the seminar industry, Dan also got to spend time with some of the world's leading marketers getting to understand how influence and persuasion works on a mass scale too.

When he isn't training sales people, Dan is an avid fitness enthusiast and regularly completes crazy fitness events for charity, including marathons, triathlons and, more recently, crossfit. He also is a huge fan of personal development and as well as regularly attending seminars is currently working on his second book based on the mindset success principles of top performing sales people.

**WWW.NEXTLEVELPERSUASION.COM**

# BONUS DOWNLOAD

I hope you enjoyed the book and have already started to apply some of the techniques in your sales process. *Next Level Persuasion* is designed to be a series of practical techniques and the sooner you start to put them into practice, the sooner you will begin to master them.

In order to help embed these lessons even further, I have put together a free bonus audio program for those of you who make it all the way through to the end of the book.

As you now know (having read the section on meta-programs) we have different preferences for learning. Reading this book will have engaged your visual and audio digital styles, and so by using a different representation system, you will be able to retain information at a different level.

Simply go to **www.NextLevelPersuasion.com/Bonus** and enter your details to get immediate access to the audio download. In it, we cover subjects such as:

**Why it is ever more important than ever to learn *Next Level Persuasion*.**

**The increasing importance of mindset and psychology in effective selling.**

**How building relationships after the sale will make you a fortune.**

You will also then be registered for the *Next Level Persuasion* newsletter which will keep you updated about events, seminars and new products that will support you in your sales career. With more books, audio programs and video trainings in development, there is plenty more still to learn.

*Here is to your continued success!*

# NEXTLEVELPERSUASION.COM/BONUS

37695264R00156

Made in the USA
Charleston, SC
18 January 2015